The History
of My Shoes
and the Evolution of
Darwin's Theory

Also by Kenny Fries

Body, Remember: A Memoir

Desert Walking: Poems

*Staring Back: The Disability Experience
From the Inside Out*

Anesthesia: Poems

The Healing Notebooks

A Human Equation

Night After Night

The History
of My Shoes
and the Evolution of
Darwin's Theory

Kenny Fries

CARROLL & GRAF PUBLISHERS

NEW YORK

Published by
Carroll & Graf
An Imprint of Avalon Publishing Group, Inc.
245 West 17th Street, 11th Floor
New York, NY 10011

AVALON
publishing group incorporated

First Carroll & Graf edition 2007

This memoir is a product of the author's recollections and is thus rendered as a subjective accounting of events that occurred in his/her life.

ISBN-13: 978-0-78672-007-1
ISBN-10: 0-7867-2007-7

9 8 7 6 5 4 3 2 1

Interior design by Maria Fernandez

Printed in the United States of America
Distributed by Publishers Group West

For Ian

your book

List of Exhibits

*No one ought to feel surprise at much remaining
as yet unexplained in regard to the origin of
species and varieties, if he makes due allowance
for our profound ignorance in regard to the
mutual relations of all the beings which live
around us.*
—Charles Darwin

*An ancient tree
Too fibrous for a logger's saw,
Too trusted to fit a carpenter's square,
Outlasts the whole forest.*
—Lao Tze

Prologue
Where Darwin Stood

We anchor in Tagus Cove off Isabela, the Galápagos island where Charles Darwin landed on September 30, 1835. Before and after Darwin, many other ships anchored here, as evidenced by the graffiti carved into the tuff: *Pike 1816, Franse 1836, Cotopaxi 1907, St. George 1924, SS Surprise 1925, Iolanda 1931.*

We climb the steep trail to what once was the crater of a volcano. Numerous lava lizards, including females that have a patch of red around their heads or necks, scamper along with us, easily making the rocky ascent past more carved graffiti.

Javier, our guide, points out the saltbush, "The plant has adapted so its leaves turn down for colder weather, and up in the heat."

Three-quarters of the way up, I need a rest. I tell Ian, who has traveled with me to the Galápagos, "I'm exhausted."

When I'm ready to continue, Ian walks in front of me. Every few steps he turns around to offer me his hand and, when needed, I reach for it and he helps pull my weight up the trail. In this way we get to the top of the ridge.

At the summit we see a lake in what was once the volcano's crater. Looking at the lake, it seems the body of water does not have an outlet to the sea. Darwin had the same thought. On a day of overpowering heat, the lake looked blue. He hurried down the cindery slope and, choked with dust, eagerly tasted the water. But to his sorrow it was brine.

Somewhere deep beneath the earth there must be a duct of some kind that allows the salt water to travel from the ocean to the lake and back again. If Darwin ever discovered such a conduit, he did not write it down. I am too tired to ask Javier how the lake, called Darwin Lake, fills with salt water. Today, it is enough that I have made it to the place where once young Darwin stood, unaware that the questions he asked about what he saw around him would change not only the course of his life but the course of what we understand about life itself.

How did I get here?

Worn dark leather molded to the contours of my feet. The sole of my right shoe slopes down gently, not quite forty-five degrees, from outer to inner edge; there is a three-inch lift attached to my right sole. The left shoe's half-inch-thick sole flat to the ground. My gait has frayed the sides of the plastic tap, strategically fastened, two to a shoe, to protect the edges of the sole.

In 1960, I was born a month premature with bones missing in both of my legs. For most of my life, when I looked at my shoes, I saw only the different way I walk.

But now when I look at my shoes I see much more than my own particular difference. I see the places they have allowed me to explore: Beehive Mountain overlooking Frenchman's Bay; Balinese jungles; the temples of Bangkok and Chiang Mai; the Colorado River rapids running through the Grand Canyon; and, especially here, the Galápagos Islands, where Charles Darwin found much to animate his theory of evolution, and where I witness a new meaning of "survival of the fittest," the phrase—often misused and misattributed to Darwin—which has haunted me since I first heard it when I was eight.

Looking at my shoes, I see Darwin's journey toward evolution, and the quest of the often forgotten Alfred Russel Wallace, cofounder of evolutionary theory, and I am deluged with images of the marine iguana and giant tortoise, the orangutan and King Bird of Paradise, the species which led these two Victorian men to change the way we think about the world and the way we live in it.

Now, finally arriving where Darwin stood, his questions have become my questions and my shoes conjure entire unseen worlds, a reimagined history informed not only by all I have seen but by all I have come to understand about chance and change, fear and transformation, variation and cultural context, ideas about the body that question the definition and existence of difference in all of our lives.

But what does any of this have to do with a pair of shoes?

Still Disabled

"Take off your shoes," Dr. Mendotti says.

For the first time in close to eight years, Social Security has decided it needs a medical review to discern if, according to their rules, I am still disabled.

Still disabled?

Specifically, I was born without fibulae, with sharp anterior curves of the tibia, and flexion contractures of the knees. Also absent were two toes and posterior calf bands on each foot. There was no scientific explanation for this situation; no medical name for the condition. Medical records simply state that I was born with "congenital deformities of the lower extremities." Despite numerous childhood surgeries, those bones are still missing—and since around the time I turned twenty-eight, because of the almost-three-inch leg length discrepancy, my increasingly weakening lower back sends a constant flow of low-grade pain throughout my body.

Dr. Mendotti's office is in Enfield, Connecticut, a half-hour drive from Northampton, Massachusetts, where I live. It is a building shared by many different doctors, more like a building housing a small town's bureaucratic departments than medical offices. The structure feels makeshift, as if these were temporary quarters until funds were raised to build a new building, but somehow as the years went on the funds never materialized. The examination room, where a secretary has placed me, looks as worn as my shoes. As worn as the disheveled, portly Dr. Mendotti, who after doing a double take at the examination room door—as though he, a specialist in the field, has never seen someone with legs and feet like mine before—has ordered me to take off my shoes, then disappeared somewhere down the hall.

Alone, I watch the clock across the room. The black second hand moves through black numbers around the unornamented white face of the institutional clock, a clock like the one in every classroom and every hall in P.S. 200, my elementary school on Benson Avenue in the Bath Beach section, between Bay Ridge and Coney Island in Brooklyn, and once again I am eight years old, staring at the P.S. 200 clock, its thin black second hand making its sixty-second round over and over and over again. In front of my third grade classroom, Mrs. Krimsky, my silver-haired teacher, is telling my class about Charles Darwin, his theory of evolution, the survival of the fittest.

At her mention of this phrase, sharp to my skin as a surgeon's knife, I instinctively reach beneath my desk and clutch my legs, protectively lifting them so my shoe-clad feet rest against the edge of my chair.

What am I afraid of? Other children's stares? Amputation? Panic-stricken, I wonder as I grow older how I will be able to walk, let alone realize my childhood dreams of becoming a basketball player, a foreign diplomat, a United States senator. Forget about dreams, with these deformed legs and feet. How will I survive?

Now, sitting in the doctor's office, I realize this clock does not tell the correct time. I know it is later than one P.M. because I left my house in Northampton at one P.M. I look at the brown, padded examination table with its familiar, unwelcoming rolled white paper to show it is clean, as well as a small black stepping stool nearby. Above, on a shelf, are five models—two white, three beige—of legs, the kind that show not only the bones, but the ligaments and tendons as well. I have always been fascinated by these models because, although I know which bones I am missing, neither my doctors nor numerous physical therapists have ever been able to tell me which ligaments and tendons my legs do contain. When I've fallen and torn something in my right knee, my doctor and I have never been sure whether it is the meniscus or the anterior cruciate ligament that I have torn, or whether it was some soft tissue adapted solely for the odd orthopedic configuration of my legs.

"Why did they send you to me?" Dr. Mendotti asks, as I take off my shoes and socks. Does he actually want me to answer?

"Wow," he breathes a mixture of pity and surprise. I wish I could recoil my legs, like the legs of the Wicked Witch of the East that curled underneath Dorothy's house which fell from the sky, when Glinda the Good Witch of the North removed the Wicked Witch's ruby slippers.

But in this situation, wanting to keep my Medicare and other benefits, I cannot curl up my legs. I must not only go through being examined by a doctor who has never seen a body like mine before, but in this situation I must act as if my disability is the worst thing that could have ever happened, when the truth is, this examination, Dr. Mendotti's stare, are much more difficult to endure.

"You can walk on those? How can I describe this to them? They won't believe me," Dr. Mendotti says, after I've given him a cursory history of the congenital deformities of my legs. "I'll have to take some photos." Decisively, he gets up, goes to the door and out into the hallway, where he talks to his secretary. "That old Polaroid must be around somewhere. You've got to come in and see this."

Dr. Mendotti returns and asks me to roll up my pants to reveal more of my legs. "You really should be using Canadian crutches to walk," he tells me.

"With the right shoes I walk just fine," I want to tell him.

"There must be doctors in Hartford who can do something for you. They work with children like you," he says.

"I'm okay as I am," I do not say.

But am I okay? This has become a recurrent question ever since, after enduring a year of back pain and knee problems, I went to see Dr. Victor Frankel, the former assistant of my childhood orthopedic surgeon.

"We can use the Ilizarov procedure," Dr. Frankel had suggested. "We cut the shell, the cortex of the bone, but leave the bone's marrow cavity, which contains important blood vessels necessary to the formation of new bone, intact. The Ilizarov apparatus consists of wires put through the bone, and external rings that are kept under a great deal of tension to apply slow traction so the nerves, muscles, tendon, and bone can grow."

As I listened to Dr. Frankel's description, my fingers reached for the four-inch scar on the right side of my knee, a remnant from the unsuccessful surgery he performed in 1966. "Theoretically, your lower back pain is caused by the length discrepancy between your legs. I can surgically line up your right foot, which now juts out from your leg at almost ninety degrees, into normal weight-bearing position, and, using the Ilizarov method, I can achieve bone growth in your right leg, making it almost as long as the left."

I have had five major reconstructive surgeries since I was born, and I did not need my searching fingers to remind me I did not want to endure another. My mind searched for an alternative. "And if I decide not to have surgery?"

"A cane would help, " Dr. Frankel offered. "I'd also suggest adding three inches to your right shoe—but only an eighth, maybe a quarter of an inch at a time, so your spine won't overcompensate. That could cause more pain and disorientation than you're experiencing now."

Seven years have passed since I rejected Dr. Frankel's surgical solution. But now, with my back pain increasing and new problems developing with my right knee and my left foot, had the time come when my asymmetrical body, with or without properly fitted shoes, had reached the apex of what it could do, of where it could take me?

Sitting in Dr. Mendotti's office, in yet another of the seemingly endless number of medical examinations, I begin to question whether or not the costs of avoiding surgery have become too great.

Dr. Mendotti takes a photo and the camera noisily releases it. From my vantage point the photo seems very yellow, as antiquated as the camera. "That should show them," he says. "Even with photographic documentation, you wouldn't believe the mistakes they make. I wish there was more I could do for you."

I smile.

Job done, Dr. Mendotti has clipped the photo to a manila folder and is now standing at the door. "If they deny you," he says with too much concern, "give me a call." The doctor pauses at the door, then he turns back to me and says: "I shouldn't say this to you, but if you ever need medication, you let me know."

I take my cane, get up, and, not paying attention to his final offer, pass the secretary's desk. I open the door and go out into what serves as the doctor's waiting room. As I make my way to my car, my limp seems more pronounced than usual.

Although the sky is full of white billowy clouds, the day seems much brighter than I remembered it an hour ago.

You can walk on those? I keep hearing Dr. Mendotti say, his words with their underlying disbelief, repeating over and over. It is as if I, too, believe that my being able to get the short way from the doctor's office to my car must be some sort of miracle. Through some act of God—not to mention doctors, shoemakers, persevering parents, and some innate drive of my own—I am able to stand here with the assistance of a cane and twenty-year-old orthopedic shoes. In this suburban world of office parks and strip malls, I am sure that if I look up I will see cherubic angels, hear them trumpeting the proof of the miracle of my being alive at all. But I don't see angels. I don't hear trumpets. Driving on I-91, I hear the words of poet Gerard Manley Hopkins: *Glory be to God for dappled things*—. I check the sky to see if it looks *couple-colored as a brinded cow*, and am thankful for Hopkins's poem celebrating *all things counter, original, spare, strange*.

But when I arrive home, I keep seeing the clock that did not tell the right time in Dr. Mendotti's office. I hear his offer of medication. Even then, I knew what he was offering, the "help" he couldn't ever voice out loud. The medication was not for pain but in case I decide that the pain is too much and I do not want to survive.

Survival of the fittest.

Somehow, I know Dr. Mendotti's reaction was not based on my pain or on my body. His reaction was based on his misunderstanding of what it means to survive in an often inhospitable world. He assumed I could not walk without crutches, although I have walked without crutches my entire life. Was Dr. Frankel's surgical solution based on the same assumptions? I have not had surgery since I was ten years old. Isn't the pain of the surgery far worse than the pain I live with now? Was I wrong to believe there had to be another way for me to adapt to my body's changes?

My childhood questions of survival are answered by Hopkins's question: how do each of us become *swift, slow; sweet, sour; adazzle, dim?* Disabled, nondisabled, I add to Hopkins's list. And I realize I am just beginning to understand what survival of the fittest actually means.

The Beehive

What is a five-foot-tall man without fibulae in both legs doing at the top of this mountain?

During my previous visit to Acadia National Park on Maine's Mount Desert Island, I became entranced with the small islands in the bay, which seemingly float in the early morning fog on what I know is water but what could be air. Since first seeing the islands in Frenchman's Bay, I have been repeating the first lines of Elizabeth Bishop's poem "North Haven"—*The islands haven't shifted since last summer, even if I like to pretend they have*—over and over again.

My boyfriend, Ian, carries the backpack that has the two bottles of water, lunch, the camera, and the guide book. Walking the first two-tenths of a mile on the flat but uneven trail, I am propelled as much by my early morning excitement as I am by my by-now deft maneuvering of my cane over larger rocks. Just a few minutes into our hike we reach the sign: BEEHIVE →.

"Here's where we make a right," I call to Ian, who is a few steps ahead of me.

"Up we go," he says when I reach him at the sign. He lets me take the lead.

Nowhere do I appreciate Ian more than when we hike together. His patience and understated cajoling have helped me reach places in Alaska and in the Canadian Rockies, as well as in Bali, I don't think I would have reached without him.

Four switchbacks later, in front of me is a small iron ladder. I count five rungs. "This should be fun," I say as I look up to plan my route.

"How do you want to do it?" Ian asks.

"You go first," I tell him, not wanting to feel the pressure of someone coming up the ladder behind me.

"And your cane?"

"I think I can pass it up to you when I'm on the first or second rung."

Climbing, I do not have trouble with heights. My challenge is to fit my right foot, jutting out at a ninety-degree angle where my ankle would be if I had one, in my bulky right shoe with its three-inch platform, securely on the ladder rung. I also need to figure out how to bear my weight since my body has changed since the last time I hiked, so, at first, I'm not sure how much either leg can bear until I try. From experience, I know that I need to do it slowly, one rung at a time, stopping on each rung to plan out my next maneuver.

As I thought, from the first rung I can pass my cane, which is not helpful in going up or down ladders, to Ian, who has bent over the side of the trail to retrieve it once he has reached the top of the ladder. Although the ladder is not long, it is narrow, making it difficult for me to fit both feet on a rung at the same time. However, the rungs are also too far apart for me to have one leg on the lower rung and the other on the next. I search the cliff in front of me for a rock

I can hold onto as I move from rung to rung. Fortunately, the hard gray granite of Mount Desert Island is suitably sturdy for me to make it up the ladder by stabilizing my body in midair with my arms, until I am able to root my foot on the next rung.

At the top of the ladder, I see another ladder, a bit longer, but similar to the one I just climbed. This time Ian hooks my cane into one of his belt loops and I climb up in the same way I climbed the first ladder.

At the top of the second ladder, I dust off my hands. Ready to take on the next challenge, I look up. Ian is staring at me.

"What's wrong?" I ask, thinking I must have dirtied myself from the climb up the first ladder.

Ian turns toward the next ladder, which is more of a cliff with metal hand holds than a ladder.

"That doesn't look too hard. I can use the hand holds for my feet," I tell him, remembering the way I made it to the cliff dwelling I wanted to see five years ago in Mesa Verde.

"How am I going to do it?" Ian asks.

"Oh," I say, too absorbed in my own thoughts on how to pass safely through this next obstacle to realize that Ian might have trouble on the trail. "I guess that's why they call it the Beehive," I offer feebly as we both look at the curving cliff on which we need to climb.

I watch Ian ascend, handhold to handhold. He slips a bit when he is unable to fit his size thirteen feet where they need to be to keep his six-foot one-inch body steady during the climb. Once he's through, I throw my cane up to the next ledge and start my ascent. Just as I thought, my feet fit easily into the handholds and I make it up this ladder more easily than the first two.

When I reach the ledge, I retrieve my cane, and make my

way up a few more switchbacks until I find Ian sitting down on a large granite boulder.

"What's the matter?" I ask, sitting next to him.

"I almost slipped on the last one. I've never been afraid of heights before," he says, gesturing his head toward the next ladder.

I walk over to where the next ascent begins. This time, not only do we have to manage the handholds on a curved cliff. This fourth ladder also turns a corner at the same time as it ascends. From where I stand I cannot see what will confront us around the bend. I have no way of knowing what the remainder of the ladder will consist of.

"We can go back," I offer, looking back at the first three ladders we climbed. They already seem stories below us.

"I don't think I can take the pack with me. It weighs me down. It feels as if it is going to pull me off the cliff."

"Okay," I say. "We can hide the pack behind the boulder. Let's drink some water now and we can have lunch on the way down."

What would Ian say when I'm having difficulty during a hike and am doubtful I can continue, the situation we usually encounter?

"Take it slow. One rung at a time. Don't look down," I offer. I don't sound convincing. "You sure you want to continue?"

"We've made it this far."

We both smile, realizing that is what I always say when trying to convince myself to continue on a hike that has become more difficult than I thought it would be.

I try to watch Ian's attempt at turning the curve. For a moment, his long body seems suspended too far from the side of the cliff and disappears around the turn.

"Are you okay?" I call out, unsure he can hear me. No response. "Ian?"

I see a leg coming around the corner where Ian, a few moments before, disappeared. The leg is followed by an unfamiliar body.

"Did you see a tall blond guy up there?" I ask.

"Yeah," the hiker tells me. "He doesn't look so good."

"What's around the corner?" I ask.

"Just the next ledge, really," he says.

"Can you do me a favor and hand me my cane when I reach the corner?"

"Sure. No problem."

When I reach the corner, the hiker hands me my cane and I nod my head to thank him. As I hoped, the next ledge is close enough to put my cane on it before I go around the bend. As I make the simultaneous ascent and turn, for once I am glad I am top heavy, because as I shift the weight from my left to right foot, one false move could topple me over into what I know is at least a three-hundred-foot drop off the side of the Beehive. My right foot fits perfectly into the top rung and I am able to swing my left leg over, lift myself up, and land kneeling on my left knee on the ledge.

I retrieve my cane and see Ian, head down, leaning against the side of the cliff. All the color has drained from his face. His chest heaves.

"You made it," I tell him. "There's only one regular ladder to go."

After I make sure he's okay, I continue up the ladder. He follows.

At the top, the Porcupine Islands—I count ten of them, each forested green on top, ringed with gray granite where it meets the sea—float before us in Frenchman's Bay.

"Drifting, in a dreamy sort of way, a little north, a little south or sidewise," I paraphrase the next lines of Bishop's poem, "they're free within the blue frontiers of bay."

The longer I look at the islands, the sky becomes the water, the water becomes the sky.

Closing my eyes, I watch the islands float before me and I see Darwin, not long after the Concepción earthquake of 1835, making his longest expedition across the Andes. Darwin reaches the crest and looks backward, astounded at the glorious view. The clear sky, an intense blue, the wild broken forms of the Cordillera Valley. The bright colored rocks contrasted with the snow-covered mountains. No plants. No birds except for a few condors flying among the peaks.

"I never thought I'd be so problematic on this hike," Ian says as we hold each against the now even stronger wind. "Sorry we don't have the camera."

"It's okay," I assure him just as he assures me when I feel my wanting to hike to these places is just a ridiculous desire, something I cannot, or should not do. "I'm sure I'll have more problems than you coming down."

But today, coming down the Beehive isn't a problem. Going down, my right shoe still fits into each ladder rung or handhold. I either pass my cane to Ian or throw it down to the next ledge. We retrieve our pack, eat lunch, and take a picture from the spot where we decided not to turn back earlier in the day.

At the bottom, as we pass the BEEHIVE → sign, I trip over a large rock that dislodged when I stepped on it. Looking down, I notice that the rock made a small gash in the leather of my right shoe.

Sitting on the side of the trail, I take off my shoes to see if the leather has been torn or whether only the polish has been rubbed off. I could not have survived the Beehive today if my shoes were any different than they are. Because of the shape of my shoes I was able to transform metal rungs stuck into the side of a cliff into footholds. Because of my shoes I was able to get to the top of the round-topped granite mountain I now see from its base.

I look at the shape of my feet—my left heel wandering to the side, my right foot jutting out at almost a right angle—so different than the way they looked ten years ago. When did the change occur? How soon before I am walking on the edges of both feet? How much longer will shoes enable me to walk? How many earthquakes did it take to change the world's surface? The granite of the Andes, seemingly so stable as the Mount Desert Island granite that enabled me to climb the Beehive, had once been as fluid as the blue water—or is it sky?—of Frenchman's Bay.

Utilitarian Shoes

Before I was ten years old, five reconstructive surgeries were performed by Dr. Joseph Milgram, the head of orthopedic surgery at the Hospital for Joint Diseases, then located in Manhattan at 125th Street and Madison Avenue. Dr. Milgram was the first doctor who did not recommend amputation of both my legs. This bespectacled doctor's doctor, by force of his gruff yet endearing personality, convinced my parents to let him begin the course of surgery that would enable their son not only to walk but to live, according to Dr. Milgram, "a normal life."

But shoes, to Dr. Milgram, were an afterthought. Early on, my mother fit me in sneakers that attached to my braces. By the time I entered kindergarten, I was able to shed my braces. I ran around like any active little boy, and my sneakers wore out on the inside edges very quickly.

By the time I was old enough to attend a full day of school, my parents realized that sneakers, even bought a dozen pair at a time, would not do the job. Before I entered first grade, at my by then semiannual appointment, they told Dr. Milgram I needed shoes. "Do you know where we can get him what he needs?" my mother asked.

Dr. Milgram, always in a hurry and usually ten thoughts ahead of everyone else, stopped short at my mother's question. Though largely responsible for my being able to walk on my own feet, it was as if he had never considered what a youngster needs to walk beyond proper weight-bearing and alignment. "Eneslow—go to Eneslow" was his mysterious command before he retreated to greet his next patient.

Not a week later, I was taken to Manhattan to see this Eneslow who had been conjured by Dr. Milgram. Eneslow, it turns out, was a shoemaker who had his office in an old narrow building with an old narrow staircase on East Fourteenth Street near Union Square. At the top of the flight of dark brown wood stairs was a dark brown wood balustrade with decorative columns, in front of a platform leading into an office lit only by the daylight that managed to make its way through an unwashed window. We went inside and Eneslow appeared from behind a curtain that led to a small back room.

This man who was to make my first pair of shoes had an unruly mop of silver-white hair and a matching mustache. He looked like a more flustered, and even more unkempt, version of Albert Einstein. The pair of shiny brown shoes he showed us cost one hundred dollars, a lot of money for the time, especially for my lower-middle-class parents. (My father was then a kosher butcher; my mother, a housewife raising my brother and me.) But the shoes were well made and, except for the heel support and the extra-thick soles that would not need to be repaired nearly as often as my sneakers, looked no different than shoes worn by the other boys I knew.

My Eneslow shoes had no left, no right; one shoe was the same shape as the other. I remember my first pair of shoes not only because, finally, like everyone else, I had shoes I could wear, but also because of the wing-tipped ornament gracing the toes, decorative like the balustrade at the top of Eneslow's staircase. My new shoes felt festive and I felt both normal *and* special.

Even though the reason for having specially made shoes was entirely utilitarian—I needed them to be able to go to school—my Eneslow shoes made me feel like Cinderella, as if during my visits to the white-haired, distracted wizard, my sneakers had been magically transformed into wing-tipped designer model shoes that, if not getting me into a prince's ball, did allow me to go to a mainstream school, a place where, at that time, children like me did not go.

marine iguana

A Little World Within Itself

"The chief sound of life here is a hiss," Herman Melville wrote of the Islas Encantadas, the Galápagos Islands. "No voice, no low, no howl is heard." These desolate islands were bypassed by such explorers as Captain James Cook, who charted the Pacific in three voyages from 1768 to 1780. George Vancouver, following up Cook's surveys in 1792, allowed his ship's naturalist Archibald Menzies to go ashore. Menzies described the island as "the most dreary, barren and desolate country I ever beheld."

Shortly after his graduation from Cambridge, twenty-two-year-old Charles Darwin began his voyage as naturalist on the HMS *Beagle* in December 1831. He did not reach the Galápagos until September 17, 1835, over half a year after he experienced the Concepción earthquake. Earlier, Darwin had read Charles Lyell's *Principles of Geology,* which put forth Lyell's idea that the process of geological elevation is piecemeal. Century after century, epoch after epoch, gradual shifts in the earth's surface slowly accumulate. After the earthquake, Darwin began considering Lyell's ideas about how millennial changes of the earth's surface affect species' survival.

Darwin's onshore Galápagos excursions were limited to only four of the islands, and did not total thirty days. His published *Beagle* diary of close to four hundred pages contains only twenty pages about the islands.

Suffering from severe seasickness, how happy Darwin must have been on land. Upon landing in the Galápagos on Chatham, now known as San Cristóbal, he found the island uninviting, mostly volcanic, consisting of black basaltic lava. Other than stunted brushwood there was little sign of life.

But Darwin also had inklings of what makes the Galápagos unique. Despite being just below the equator, the islands' climate is not excessively hot, which he suspected could be because of the low temperature of the surrounding sea. Except during one short season, little rain falls in the archipelago, but the clouds generally hang low. A large number of the Galápagos's plants and animals could be found nowhere else. Once, a mockingbird landed on Darwin's water pitcher. He noticed the bird was tame and unsuspecting of him, not even understanding when he threw stones at it. The birds came so close that they could easily be killed by a stick.

On Chatham Island, Darwin encountered two giant tortoises, each weighing at least two hundred pounds, eating a piece of cactus. When he approached, one of the prehistoric tortoises looked at him, then quietly walked away; the other hissed deeply and drew in its head.

On Albemarle (Isabela) Island, Darwin was introduced to the marine iguana, a hideous-looking black lizard between three and four feet long. When on land, the creature moved stupidly and sluggishly. However, when in the water, the iguana swam with perfect ease and quickness, using a serpentine movement of its body and flattened tail. Its limbs and strong claws are well adapted to crawl over the jagged lava of the coast. Yet, when swimming, its legs are motionless, collapsed closely to its sides. After capturing a few of the creatures and cutting open their stomachs, Darwin realized that marine iguanas do not eat fish, but rather sea algae and other seaweed. When he threw one of the marine iguanas into the ocean it quickly retreated to land, from which he speculated that their predators, such as sharks, must be aquatic.

On Albemarle, Darwin made another observation: the beaks of the various finches on the island range "from one exceeding in dimension that of the largest gros-beak, to another differing but little from that of a warbler."

On James (Santiago) Island, Darwin saw a different lizard with a dirty-yellowish-orange belly, front legs, and head, and a crown that was nearly white. The back of the lizard was brownish red, and darker in the younger ones. These creatures weighed as much as fifteen pounds and seemed unusually lazy, almost torpid. This is the land iguana of James Island. The land iguana eats the fruit of the succulent cactus, which has been blown off by the wind. Darwin found this species of land iguanas confined solely to the central islands, to him a logical distribution as land iguanas, unlike marine iguanas, cannot disperse themselves by swimming to the outlying islands of the archipelago.

Darwin was haunted by all of this, admitting, "It never occurred to me that the productions of islands only a few miles apart, and placed under the same physical conditions, would be dissimilar."

Bodies of Water

Sitting at the edge of my local YMCA pool, I think again of Hopkins's question: *swift, slow; sweet, sour; adazzle, dim . . . fickle, freckled, who knows how?* I rock back and forth, feel the rough, stuccoed cement chafe the back of my thighs.

Unlike the pool at Lansman's Bungalow Colony in the Catskills in upstate New York, where my family spent thirteen of my childhood summers, there are no comforting steps leading down into this water, just two silver-gray metal holds one above the other—not even a ladder—on each side of the pool's shallow end. There is no way to ease in, body part by body part, ever so slowly, as I have been doing ever since I learned to swim.

I close my eyes and imagine I am swimming like the lone other swimmer in the pool this morning. I imagine the water against his body as he glides, hand over head, hand over head, one stroke after the next, until he reaches the other end of the pool. Swimming, back stretched, no pressure on my legs, the water neutralizing weight, is easier for me than walking.

With my palms, I spread water on my thighs. The fingers on my left hand gently knead my left thigh. When has this thigh developed so much muscle? Bending my knee, I stretch out my left leg its entire twenty-two-inch length and notice, as if for the first time, how the ligament running up my leg on the outside between my knee and thigh will not fully extend. Three inches longer than my right leg, my left leg never has the opportunity to reach its potential elongation.

My left leg outstretched over the shallow end of the pool, I begin to run my hand from sole to hip, the entire length of my leg. The lone swimmer, having finished his laps, grabs for a metal rung and lifts himself out of the pool. I watch the water drip from his well-toned chest, from his washboard stomach, his sculpted thighs, forming a substantial puddle on the floor.

Above the hips my body could be described just like everybody else's. *Your body—okay, at least your upper parts—can look like his.*

The comparison to the now-departed swimmer does the trick, and in one motion I am skimming the water's surface, making my way up the length of the pool. But as I move my body through the water I am reminded that I do not swim correctly. Afraid the chlorine will sting my allergy-ridden eyes, never sure how to breathe smoothly, holding my breath when under water, releasing my breath when above, when swimming I keep my head out of the water. My feet, for years strong enough to perform daily tasks, and to travel, do not have a propulsive kick when swimming, leaving the bulk of my body's water work to my arms and upper torso.

Lap 20. I think about the idea of normal in relation to the well-toned swimmer who by now, having showered, I imagine is in the locker room drying his naked body. When imagining this naked man I also imagine myself among the men in the locker room who are surreptitiously, some more overtly, gazing at this man's beauty. And by such a measuring gaze, disabled and nondisabled, designate ourselves as *other*, the beautiful man as the *norm*, if not some unreachable Greek ideal. Some of us spend our entire lives as the beholder, the one who gazes, trying to achieve for ourselves this abstract, ultimately fictitious notion of what we should be, an ideal which being a projection—*if, if, only if*—evaporates as if it were the water of which our bodies, and the world in which our bodies inhabit, are mostly comprised.

Lap 30. One more lap and my swim will be over. I do not use the metal rungs at the side of the pool. With my palms flat against the surface where only an hour ago I sat on the edge of the pool, I lift myself from the water.

As I make my way from the pool into the shower I think about my travels, my personal history in relation to the fantasy of the ideal, the reality that can never be the norm. With all these thoughts moving fast through my mind it is as if I am still weightless.

When I was in my early twenties, when I was a graduate student in New York, as well as during my first years after graduate school living in San Francisco, I had success finding sexual partners in bars. When I first started going to bars I planted myself at a table or on a stool at the bar and stayed in one place as long as possible. When I saw someone I wanted to get to know, I stayed put, as frozen to the barstool as I was this morning to the concrete edge of the YMCA pool. Even when I had to go to the bathroom I put it off for as long as I could to avoid making my disability noticeable by standing up and walking around the bar. By deciding to remain stationary, to my mind I made myself nondisabled. As soon as I walked I felt I would become disabled.

Only once during my years of going to the bars did a man decide not to go home with me after he noticed my legs. That one time, after I had been talking with this guy most of the evening, long after it had become obvious we would leave the bar together and go back to where one of us lived, when I got up and he saw that I stood just over five feet tall, he immediately decided not to leave the bar with me. When I stood up, this man who a moment before had been running his finger up and down the length of my arm, became flustered and without saying a word walked to the other side of the bar. As far as I know, only this once in my years of going to bars were my legs actually a disability. And what made me disabled was not my bodily impairment but this man who decided to disable my body by choosing, for whatever reasons that were his own, not to have sex with me that night. Isn't it true that a dark-haired man who is rejected by a potential partner who is attracted only to blonds is, in that situation, disabled by another's predilections and not by the color of his hair?

Crucial to this understanding is: What is a disability? Who is disabled? Who decides? Sometimes, as was my experience with that man in that bar, the decision is made by someone who seizes the power of naming. And, at other times, I have to admit, the disabling agent has been none other than myself.

No longer drinking alcohol, allergic to smoky places, and no longer interested in meeting men this way, I stopped going to bars. When I moved to Northampton, I found out my cholesterol was way too high and my doctor recommended I swim for cardiovascular exercise. So I joined the YMCA, which had a good pool and was close to where I lived.

During the late morning and early afternoon, the YMCA is nearly empty. Most who use the facilities during these hours are elderly Eastern European men. Long dormant hybrid languages of the recent past are whispered in the locker room and showers.

When I began my cholesterol-lowering regimen, I noticed a few men my age who swam every other day the same time as I did. After my almost-an-hour swim, in the showers or in the locker room, I was surprised that many of these men took an obviously sexual interest in me. Why in bars where I was fully clothed did I usually go unnoticed, but when my lower body was revealed naked in the showers at the YMCA did men consistently pursue me? Were my expectations of how men react to my disability that out of line? Had I internalized all the negative body imagery, the stereotypes, the fear of disability to the point where I could no longer think clearly about the effect my body's difference had in the world?

When I reach the showers, the swimmer with whom I compared myself is gone. Through the spraying water, I hear Gerard Manley Hopkins's question—*fickle, freckled, who knows how?*—and staring down at my feet, my childhood question— why was I born missing bones in my both of my legs?— returns. Why was it so difficult for me to realize that I could compete successfully—indeed, survive—in this overtly physical world? Why do each of us spend so much of our resources on changing what we look like, changing who we are? And, as if in answer, I speak Hopkins's words: *All of our beauty should be past change.*

Darwin's Downe House

Darwin at Home

In 1836, Darwin returned from his *Beagle* voyage and reentered the privileged world of the Victorian gentry not as the clergyman he thought he would be, but as a gentleman-naturalist. He married his first cousin, the religiously devout Emma Wedgwood. The Darwins had two children, William, born in 1839, and Anne, born in 1841.

Besides publishing his *Beagle* diaries and other works on geology, he spent much of his time farming out his specimen collections to experts who could properly classify what he had brought home from his five-year voyage.

In 1838, Darwin began reading Thomas Robert Malthus's "Essay on the Principle of Population." In this 1798 essay, Malthus states that despite the human capability to double their numbers over a twenty-five-year period, the number of individuals living at one time seemed to be broadly balanced with the means of subsistence. The reason Malthus gives for this are "checks" on the increase of populations. In one category he puts "positive checks" such as early death, disease, famine, epidemics, and war. There are also "preventative checks," such as late marriage, sexual abstinence, and moral restraint, as well as what he deemed "unnatural practices" such as abortion and infanticide.

In September 1838, Darwin, while reading Malthus, thought about his *Beagle* voyage. He realized that what Malthus said about checks in the human world also held true for animals and plants: "One may say there is a force like a hundred thousand wedges trying [to] force every kind of adapted structure into the gaps in the economy of nature, or rather forming gaps by thrusting out weaker ones. The final cause of all this wedgings [*sic*], must be to sort out proper structure & adapt it to change." Darwin recognized that he now had a system to explain how adaptations continue to thrive as unadaptive species, one by one, die out, resulting in each prospering species becoming increasingly better adapted to external conditions.

Darwin's study of the breeding of domesticated plant and animal species solidified his theory. He found that wild species are created by the same process as domesticated ones, only infinitely slower.

Since his return from the *Beagle* voyage, he had been vexed by questions about the distribution of species: Why are animals on islands so different from those on the nearest mainland? Why were the fossils he found in Patagonia so similar to what currently lived in Patagonia? Why does each island of an archipelago have its own endemic species that are more similar to each other than to related species farther away? What is the origin of species?

By October 1838, he had consolidated his theory, using what he had learned about geology. This theory of "gradualism" made colleagues, such as the *Beagle*'s Captain FitzRoy, realize Darwin was in the process of transforming the earth's history into an entirely secular story.

Darwin's work on barnacles, their sexual reproduction, and its relationship to variation, took him eight years to complete. This crucial work made him realize that variation was a natural consequence of reproduction. His emphasis on Lyellian geology, the slow accumulation of gradual shifts in the earth's surface, which put the constantly changing earth at the core, was now being replaced by the mechanism of species variation.

As a member of the very society his theory of evolution was sure to shock, and husband to the religiously devout Emma, Darwin took great pains to make sure he had amassed all the necessary proof before he went public with his theory. He began to suffer stomach problems. "Unusually unwell, swimming head, depression, trembling, many bad attacks of sickness," he wrote in October 1848. In November, he missed his father's funeral: "I was at the time unwell that I was unable to travel which added to my misery." At the end of 1849: "My stomach fails so often & so suddenly that I am never certain of an appointment." Were the increasing pain and exhaustion related to what he increasingly knew would turn the world upside down?

Despite knowing others were thinking similar ideas about evolution, he could not speed up his work. He was ruled by his body.

In 1851, Darwin's favorite child, Anne, died of scarlet fever. She was ten. Anne's death made him revisit Malthus's theory of "checks" on population. Despite Darwin's idea of "the invisible hand"—the name he had given to his yet unnamed theory of the selection of who will live and who will die—he knew that for his theory of selection to work, a large part of the process had to be governed by chance. Why did his beloved daughter get scarlet fever? Why not his son William? Why not Darwin himself?

I.D. Shoes

I see my shoes on the floor by my bed. I spot the place on the right shoe where the polish was rubbed off, the leather nearly torn by my misstep while hiking down the Beehive. Before the tear gets deeper, I will have to send the shoe to Frank, the cobbler, to be repaired.

One Friday when I was ten, I asked my mother if instead of taking the bus home from school, would she pick me up so I could go with her to bring my shoes to Frank's shop, which I had never seen before.

"And how do you plan to get home without your shoes?" she asked me rhetorically, moving her face toward mine with a familiar look, which to this day remains a perfect combination of amusement and disapproval.

"You can bring the stroller," I replied triumphantly.

Up three small steps from the street, Frank's storefront shop was only slightly less narrow than the staircase that led up to Eneslow's. The shop's walls were lined with shelves filled with what seemed like hundreds of pairs of leather shoes. Everything in the shop was dark, even Frank's thin mustache, as well as the wood counter that looked more like what might be found in a corner bar. The counter had a section that could be lifted up on hinges, not unlike the drawbridge we passed on the way to visit my maternal grandparents in Far Rockaway every other Sunday. The machine on which Frank's son Michael, his assistant, cobbled a well-worn shoe, had been painted black, making it look similar to my other, Orthodox Jewish grandmother's ancient Singer sewing machine that dominated her bedroom in her Borough Park apartment.

But what most dominated Frank's shop on Harway Avenue was shoe polish, which I remember as smelling something like horses. The scent, combined with the earthy colors, made the shop feel safe, like home. Not the homeyness associated with heavy curtains or upholstered chairs, but the masculine solidity of a bookshelf-lined study or a firm hug from my father.

My feet continued to change to the point that my old Eneslow shoes, a new pair bought every two years, did not fit. Not only did the soles wear out too quickly, but my surgically reconstructed right foot now jutted out at an almost forty-five-degree angle from what would have been my ankle, if I had one. By 1970, the last operation on my legs completed, I needed two distinctly shaped, differentiated shoes. In May, at my now-yearly appointment with Dr. Milgram, my mother asked him, "What can we do?"

This time Dr. Milgram seemed prepared. "Give them Jerry Miller's card," the doctor told Alice, his secretary.

"Let me see it," I asked my mother as we were stuck in traffic on the FDR Drive on the ride home from Manhattan. On the card was a logo that, even though shaped like a sole of a shoe, looked like the enlarged fingerprint on the cover of a mystery novel I had read.

A few weeks later, after school I took the train into Manhattan to meet my father, who was coming from his job in New Jersey, at the storefront office of Jerry Miller I.D. Shoes on East Twenty-ninth Street, just off Park Avenue South. Waiting, I stared in the large window at the shoes, each distinctly shaped, each a different color—black, beige, even green and red, as well as the customary brown. In the store I saw an elderly man and woman get up from their metal folding chairs. Soon, they came out the door, each holding a box that I imagined contained a pair of their own personal I.D. shoes. I saw my father coming down the street. Together we went inside.

Jerry Miller, much younger than both Dr. Milgram, then in his midseventies, and Eneslow, who was at least as old as Dr. Milgram, shook both my father's hand and mine. Jerry Miller seemed more affable and contemporary compared to my bow-tie-clad doctor and the wizardish Eneslow. He reminded me of the salesman who sold my father his used emerald green Buick the summer before. "Get on up there," Jerry Miller said, beckoning me to a platform not unlike those used by shoeshine men I had seen in the Times Square subway station.

"Take off your shoes and socks," he told me, and after I did he rolled my jeans all the way up to my knees. I watched Jerry Miller prepare the plaster he would use to make a mold of my feet and I remembered how my father had to learn how to replaster my casts when I, as a young boy, recuperated from surgery. "You can probably teach him how to do it," I said proudly to my father who from the other side of the small room was watching Jerry Miller's plaster preparations.

My tired feet felt warm and comfortable, safe in the plaster casts Jerry Miller molded to send to the factory in Athol, Massachusetts, where my shoes would actually be made. My muscles relaxed as if my feet were in a hot bath after a long day's hike.

Involuntarily, my body jumped when I saw the blade. Jerry Miller turned on the plaster-cutting electric saw he needed to cut the casts to separate them from my feet and lower legs. I winced at the grating metallic noise that had accompanied every removal of every cast I had ever worn.

This shrill, reverberating noise intensified my fear that the blade would cut through the plaster, pierce my skin, my bone, and amputate my leg. I closed my eyes but still I could not stop thinking how in one quick moment my feet could be gone—and I would never have legs again. What need of shoes then?

My skin felt ice cold. Instinctively, I reached down to scratch my right leg and half of the cast was already resting in Jerry Miller's palm. With one quick flick of his wrist he had removed the rest of the cast from my left leg. By the time my skin adjusted to the room's temperature, the painful separation of plaster from leg hair was over. My skin tingled. I picked at the tiny bits of plaster still attached to my leg hairs. I wiggled my toes and stretched my feet up and down, from side to side, and watched Jerry Miller mark up the casts, which looked like my feet and lower legs.

After dipping my feet in warm water to dissolve the plaster still stuck on my legs, I put on my socks, then shoes, and watched Jerry Miller place my casts in a padded mailing box.

"What color?" Jerry Miller asked.

"Brown, like my old shoes," I told him.

"We should have them in less than a month," he said. "I've put a rush on them."

I looked down at my old shoes as I walked with my father west on East Twenty-ninth Street and north up Lexington Avenue toward the subway. Walking down the steps to catch the train, I thought how magical it seemed when every two years Eneslow retrieved my new pair of shoes from the closet where he stored his wizard's wares. This new process was not as magical, seemed to defy the mystery of the soleprint logo on Jerry Miller's card.

On the subway platform, I could not get the sound of the plaster-cutting saw out of my head. The train screeched to a halt, its wheels the sound of imminent amputation.

Amazon parrot

Wallace in the Amazon

In 1835, when Darwin toiled in the Galápagos, Alfred Russel Wallace was twelve. Two years later, Wallace's parents lost their financial legacy and could no longer afford his education. Wallace began an apprenticeship as a surveyor, working and living with his older brother, William, in London.

In 1838, Wallace, while studying at the mechanic's institute at Kington, wrote a paper arguing that science should have a primary place within the institute. Preparing this paper, he came into contact with many of the leading scientific journals and texts of the time, including Lyell's *Principles of Geology*.

Three years later, Wallace took up astronomy using a home-made telescope. By 1842, he became interested in botany, eventually reading Lindley's *Elements of Botany* and a borrowed copy of Loudon's *Encyclopedia of Plants*. Into his copy of Lindley's text, Wallace copied the following passage from Darwin's *Journal of the Voyage of the Beagle*: "I am strongly induced to believe that as in music, the person who understands every note will if he also possesses a proper taste, more thoroughly enjoy the whole, so he who examines each part of a fine view may also thoroughly comprehend the full and combined effect. Hence, a traveller should be a <u>Botanist</u>, for in all views plants form the chief embellishment." He began his own herbarium, learning how to dry specimens and identify what he collected on his mountain walks.

Unable to make a life as a surveyor or a teacher, Wallace, in 1848, investigated the possibilities of earning a living in the specimens trade. Inspired by reading William Edwards's popular *A Voyage up the Amazon,* Wallace set sail for the Amazon on April 26, 1848, as a twenty-five-year-old self-taught naturalist on the barge *Mischief.*

Thirty-two days later, the *Mischief* landed at Pará, Brazil, at the mouth of the Amazon River. Wallace was disappointed that Pará did not have the spectacular birds or diversity of butterflies he had expected. His first trip upriver, to Tocantins, gave him a taste for collecting in the jungle. He decided to move his base upriver.

During the first year alone on his Amazon adventure, Wallace, who had been amassing a valuable collection of birds, including the highly prized white umbrella bird, plants, insects, and butterflies, began to imagine himself as more than a collector. He marveled at how well adapted the animals were to their food and habitat, and began to look for a principle regulating the infinitely varied forms of animal life. He planned a set of books based on his journals and observations.

His younger brother, Herbert, sailed to Brazil on June 7, 1849, and briefly joined Wallace upriver. In December 1851, Wallace, still in the jungle, received a letter telling him that Herbert had died of yellow fever in Pará in June. Feeling ill himself and worrying that he, too, would succumb to yellow fever, Wallace decided to cut his losses and head back to Pará with his dwindling collection: five monkeys, two macaws, twenty parrots, a white-crested pheasant, a few smaller birds, and a toucan. The night before he sailed, the toucan flew away and drowned.

Arriving in Pará, where yellow fever was still running rampant, Wallace immediately booked his passage back to England, but managed to visit Herbert's grave. On July 12, 1852, he set sail on a brig with what remained of his collection.

Two days at sea, the ship's captain searched for Wallace after breakfast. "I'm afraid the ship's on fire," the captain told him. "Come and see what you think of it."

Smoke engulfed the inside of the ship. Wallace quickly gathered up what he could: a tin box with a couple of shirts, into which he put his drawings of fish and palms, and his watch. All on board took to the lifeboats, from which they watched the boat go up in flames. One parrot fell into the water and was picked up, the only remaining species Wallace was able to take back with him to England. His Amazon journey had lasted four years.

Despite the loss of his specimen collections and two years of journals in the fire, Alfred Russel Wallace persevered. In March 1854, two years after returning to England, he embarked on his next journey, this time to the Spice Islands of the Malay Archipelago, now part of Indonesia.

Bali starling

Echoes of Extinction

From the moment I saw its photo in the travel guide I knew I had to see it: *Leucopsar rothschildi,* otherwise known as the Bali starling. Months before, when planning our trip to Bali, I asked Ian to draw me a picture of the nearly extinct creature small enough to be held in the palm of a hand, a bird with white plumage and a turquoise mask, one of only two subspecies exclusive to this Indonesian island, the other being the now-extinct Bali tiger.

Unusual for a bird, a Bali starling does not like to get wet. The rain startles the small bird and, when wet, it does not move. The locals know that when it rains the starling is ripe for capture. Over the years, as their number declined, the value of these small creatures rose astronomically. As so often happens, their value increased their rate of destruction.

Up at dawn, we are driven by our guide from our hotel to the Bali Starling Reintroduction Center, part of Bali Barat National Park, in the northwestern corner of the island. The reintroduction center is now the only place to see the endangered bird in its natural habitat.

On our way to the center, I take Ian's drawing out of my journal. Looking at his version of the Bali starling, I think about the numerous, mostly comic, depictions of *Raphus cucullatus,* commonly known as the dodo, a large flightless species of pigeon once unique to the island of Mauritius.

Portuguese sailors were the first Westerners to reach Mauritius, in 1507. A journal from 1607 talks of the men living on "Tortoises, Dodos, Pigeons, Turtle-doves, grey Parrots and other game," which were caught by hand in the woods. The dodos, like the Galápagos tortoises, proved a very useful source of fresh meat for European sailors.

Hunting by humans played a large role in the decline of the dodo population, but it is only part of the story. The introduction to Mauritius by the Portuguese, and later the Dutch, of pigs and monkeys, deadly predators of the flightless dodo's juveniles and nests, sealed the dodo's fate.

The last credible eyewitness account of living dodos is from 1662, when Volquard Iversen, a Dutchman, was marooned on Mauritius after being shipwrecked in a storm. By 1667, there were no dodos left on Mauritius, no dodos left in the world.

Prior to the arrival of the Europeans, after many thousands of years on Mauritius, the dodo had adapted itself well to the local conditions of the island. By evolutionary standards, the dodo was a success.

But on an island with no large predators the dodo also grew to become, like many species on the Galápagos Islands, "ecologically naive." The dodo, like the marine iguanas, the giant tortoises, and the mockingbird that Darwin tells us perched on his water pitcher, adapted to this absence of land predators. These seemingly tame animals did not know fear.

Then, confronted with what the progress of civilization had to offer—disease as well as scientific and technical advancement—were these species able to relearn the instinct of fear? Did this instinct lie dormant in them until it was reactivated by the new, threatening situation? Or did they have to learn this fear all over again as if it had never been felt before?

Did the absence of fear make these species easy prey for the newly arrived humans and the newly arrived germs they brought with them? Or did this absence of fear allow the humans a closer look to learn about the species and perhaps ensure their long-term survival? What role does progress play in our understanding of species different from our own? What role does fear play in how we think and act in the presence of variation?

Orangutan

What Wallace Found

"If we look at a globe or a map of the Eastern hemisphere," wrote Alfred Russel Wallace, "we shall perceive between Asia and Australia a number of large and small islands, forming a connected group distinct from those of great masses of land, and having little connexion with either of them." The Spice Islands, now largely known as Indonesia, are situated on the equator, surrounded by the warm tropical oceans. Wallace considered the region more hot and moist than any other part of the globe, teeming with collectible plants and animals that were elsewhere unknown.

Arriving in April 1854, Wallace used Singapore as a base, learning about his new environment and collecting beetles and butterflies. During the evenings, he began to make notes for a book he intended to call "The Organic Law of Change." In search of birds and animals, he made expeditions north to the Malay Peninsula, to Malacca, where he contracted malaria. After several months of recuperation, Wallace took up the offer of Sir Edward Brooke, the Rajah of Sarawak, and, in November

1854, moved his base to Borneo, eight hundred miles northwest of Bali.

During the rainy first months of 1855, Wallace, once again beset by malaria, holed up in a bungalow lent to him by Rajah Brooke, by the mouth of the Sarawak River, at the foot of Santubong Mountain. There he wrote the first section of the book he began in Singapore. In this paper, "On the Law Which Has Regulated the Introduction of New Species," Wallace derived some of his main argument from a passage in Darwin's *Voyage of the Beagle:*

> The Galapagos are a volcanic group of high antiquity, and have probably never been more closely connected with the continent than they are at present. They must have been first peopled, like other newly formed islands, by the action of winds and currents, and at a period sufficiently remote to have had the original species die out, and the modified prototypes only remain. In the same way we can account for the separate islands having each their peculiar species, either on the supposition that the same original emigration peopled the whole of the islands with the same species from which differently modified prototypes were created, or that the islands were successively peopled from each other, but that new species have been created in each on the plan of the pre-existing ones.

This Sarawak paper goes further than Darwin's *Beagle* diary. Wallace describes why the direct lineage from species to species is so difficult to determine: "[W]e have only fragments of this vast system, the stem and main branches being represented by extinct species of which we have no knowledge, while a vast mass of limbs and boughs and minute twigs and scattered leaves is what we have to place in order. . . ."

In Borneo, Wallace wanted to see an orangutan. Not only was he interested in studying an orangutan's habits but he also wanted to collect this highly prized specimen for sale back in England. He saw no contradiction in doing both.

Once he recovered from his latest bout with malaria, the abundance of orangutans near the Sarawak allowed him to shoot fifteen between January and June 1855. On one expedition he rescued a baby orangutan, only about a foot long, found hanging on to its mother when Wallace killed her. The baby orangutan had not been wounded. Still strong and active, it began to cry when Wallace cleaned the mud out of its mouth.

Taking the baby orangutan into his jungle cabin, Wallace fed it rice water from a bottle with a quill in the cork. The baby orangutan, by trial and error, learned to suck from the bottle. Wallace added sugar and coconut milk to the formula, attempting to make the liquid diet more nourishing.

After five weeks the baby orangutan had not grown or gained weight. Soon it became ill, lost all appetite, and died.

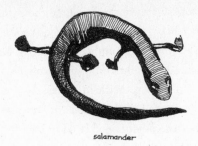

salamander

My Salamanders

Even though my childhood summers were cooler in the Catskills than in our fifteenth-floor apartment in Brooklyn, for an inevitable week toward the end of July during the summer there was a stretch of unrelenting heat and stifling humidity. The heat wave was always ended by an intense storm, as if all our pent-up frustration with the inexorable heat and humidity was unleashed in the torrential rain that pelted the roof, pounded the path and porch outside our bungalow, and dripped from the screen windows onto the windowsills and into our kitchen through the front screen door.

I loved this rain and the near-deafening sound it made on the roof, porch, and pathway, not only because I knew my allergies would abate when the storm ended the heat wave. I loved this rain because after it rained I would be able to roam the dense woods behind the bungalows and hunt for salamanders.

I went salamander hunting with my friend Paul, whose family had an upstairs bungalow beyond third base of the softball field across the road. It was midmorning when we made our way with our empty Tupperware containers along the path littered with worms unearthed by the rain. The woods were damp and even the slightest breeze brought large drops of water down from the leaves and branches onto our heads.

At first it was difficult to adjust to the darkness of the woods. And when our eyes adjusted to the woods, it was still difficult to spy a salamander that camouflaged itself to look the color of the brown dirt or the velvety green moss. But soon Paul was yelling, "Salamander! Salamander!" and then I was yelling "Salamander!" too, and by lunchtime, when we ended our hunt, Paul and I had filled two large containers with the helpless slimy amphibians. Back in my bungalow we transferred our catch to a larger plastic container that we lined with earth, rocks, and moss to create for the salamanders a habitat that approximated their own.

I fed my salamanders with leaves and dead bugs I found beneath the yellow bug traps my mother hung in the corner of the porch.

A week later, I raced with my container to the porch and, opening it, found my salamanders, close to fifty of them, rigid inside. They looked like those lifeless dioramas I'd built numerous times for school homework assignments. But the awful sour smell that emanated from the container reminded me that this was no diorama, these lifeless creatures were once alive.

I dropped the container and ran screaming inside, where I kept jumping up and down. I could not calm down enough to tell my mother why I was so disturbed. She had to go outside to see for herself what caused her young son to become so distraught.

"How long have they been that way?" I asked her when she returned inside.

"How am I supposed to know? They can't live long out of the woods," my mother said.

Later, as I buried my salamanders under a tree behind the bungalow, I apologized to each and every one, vowing never to remove another living creature from its natural home.

king bird of paradise

Birds of Paradise

Back in England, Wallace's Sarawak paper was published in September 1855. He received little reaction.

In the margins of his copy, Darwin wrote: "Nothing very new—uses my simile of the tree—It seems all creation with him." But Lyell and others urged him to take another look. Rereading the paper, Darwin realized Wallace was about to preempt him: "Began by Lyell's advice writing species sketch. . . . I am like Croesus overwhelmed with my riches in facts & I mean to make my book as perfect as ever I can." Darwin decided to call his book *Natural Selection*.

As 1855 drew to a close, Wallace spent time with Rajah Brooke while waiting for a boat to Singapore. Brooke's secretary recalls Wallace's sharing his initial thoughts on how orangutans might be human ancestors. That December, Wallace received his first correspondence from Darwin: a list of species he wanted Wallace to collect for him. Wallace finally sailed to Singapore on January 25, 1856. There, he waited four months for funds from the sale in England of his collection of insects. He was now able to plan his next expedition to the town of Macassar, on Celebes, the large island east of Borneo.

On his way to Macassar, Wallace stopped briefly at Bali and Lombok. He observed that one species of cockatoo was abundant in Lombok but not found in Bali. Wallace realized that Lombok formed the western boundary of the range of not only this species but all cockatoos. In doing so, he had deduced the dividing line between the Asian and Australian biospheres, a discovery that would prove to be of major importance in his ideas about species distribution and evolution.

Wallace arrived in Macassar in September 1856, and once again became ill with malaria. When he recovered the following January, he moved to Dobbo, a trading settlement. His new goal was to find the king bird of paradise.

After several days, Baderoon, one of his native assistants, brought him a small bird:

> The greatest part of its plumage was of an intense cinnabar red, with a gloss as of spun glass. On the head the feathers became short and velvety, and shaded into rich orange. Beneath, from the breast downward, was pure white, with the softness and gloss of silk, and across the breast a band of deep metallic green; the bill was yellow, and the feet and legs were of a fine cobalt blue, strikingly contrasting with all the other parts of the body. . . . Springing from each side of the breast, and ordinarily lying concealed under the wings, were little tufts of greyish feathers about two inches long, and each terminated by a broad band of intense emerald green. These plumes can be raised at will by the bird, and spread out into a pair of elegant fans when

the wings are elevated. . . . The two middle feathers
of the tail are in the form of slender wires about five
inches long, and which diverge in a beautiful
double curve. About half an inch of the end of this
wire is webbed on the outer side only, and coloured
of a fine metallic green, and being curled spirally
inward, form a pair of elegant glittering buttons,
hanging five inches below the body, and the same
distance apart.

Wallace went on to describe: "These two ornaments, the
breast fans and the spiral-tipped tailwires are altogether
unique, not occurring on any other species of the eight thousand different birds that are known to exist upon the earth;
and, combined with the most exquisite beauty of plumage,
render this one of the most perfectly lovely of the many lovely
productions of nature."

Seeing the rare beautiful bird, Wallace imagined how year
by year these creatures were born, lived, and died amid the vir-
ginal Dobbo forests where few humans could gaze upon their
beauty. He instinctively understood a paradox: because of their
isolation these birds would go unnoticed but, if "civilization"
ever reached these islands, the balanced relation between the
bird and its environment would be disturbed. The result would
be the decline and, finally, the extinction of these wondrous
creatures whose structure and beauty man alone could appreciate and enjoy.

Bananas and Dew

The car has stopped and our guide leads us through the dense jungle. Usually, when walking with others, I am at least a few steps behind my companions. But this morning I cannot contain my excitement—never before have I seen an endangered species—and it is difficult for me not to overtake Ian and our guide. As I wait for them, impatiently, at the entrance to the reintroduction center, I feel the first drops of what might be rain.

A short way from the gate, I see the cages. Then I make out a white starling, and another. I get near enough to see their exquisite turquoise masks. Looking closely at their faces, set against the pure white feathers, it is as if each turquoise band has been individually, painstakingly painted by hand.

In the corner of the cage, I notice an upright object. I look questioningly at our guide. "Banana?" I ask him.

"Yes, yes, banana."

"They survive on bananas and dew," Ian says, coming up behind me.

"I can't believe these small birds can survive in the jungle."

"What about the moths?" Ian asks.

"What moths?"

"I read about it in *National Geographic*. It's a recent example of evolution by natural selection," Ian tells me. "In industrial England, pale white moths were easily seen on trees darkened by smoke. A rare mutant moth was darker, closer to the color of the tree bark, so it was not as easily caught by birds. Over time, the tree trunks became darker from air pollution and the mutant genes spread. The pale moths were mostly replaced by the darker ones."

Ian's story of the white moths' disappearance reminds me that, just like the fate of the dodo, "survival of the fittest" is only part of the story. A gene or an individual cannot be called "fit" in isolation but only in the context of a particular environment.

Our guide takes us inside a dilapidated hut, which serves as the administrative hub of the center. Inside, there is access to other fenced-in areas, with two starlings in each cage. In the narrow hall are small wooden carts with wooden boxes on top.

"Look in the box," our guide tells us.

Inside the box is the tiniest bird I have ever seen. It looks more like an embryo than a bird, its beak seemingly larger than the rest of its colorless body. Thinking we are here to feed it, the embryo-like creature opens its beak, pleading.

Immediately, I go back outside.

"What's the matter?" Ian asks, trailing behind me.

When I turn to him, he embraces me.

"Incubator," is all I can say to him. This one word is enough. Ian knows that, because I was born a month premature, I spent the first four weeks of my life in an incubator. The doctors were not sure whether I would live.

On the way back to our hotel, I am silent in the backseat of the car. But my mind is anything but silent. I am still surprised at my reaction to the small embryo-like starling who opened its mouth to us as if its life depended on our decision whether to give what it needs to survive.

Ambulatory People

"It happened by chance," lawyer Lisa Blumberg writes in the current issue of *The Disability Rag*.

When a child, because of cerebral palsy, Lisa walked with her "arms flying, knock kneed, right leg turned in, about half the speed of an ordinary person."

Lisa's parents moved the family from New Jersey, where she had a doctor who saw her as a whole person, to Boston, where she saw a doctor who wanted to fix her. She was about to go to college. Her parents panicked.

When Lisa's parents first took her to the Boston doctor he complimented them. "I see you've been able to do some things with her. Good for you," the young doctor, dressed in a white jacket, told Lisa's parents. "Now, we have to think of her future. Her adductors are tight. They are going to get tighter and tighter, and, by the time she's sixty or seventy, her hips will dislocate. She should have an adductor myotomy."

After surgery, Lisa could never walk again as easily and pain-free as she had before she moved to Boston. Close to twenty years and many physical therapists later, Lisa, now a lawyer, wrote to a famous Swiss orthopedist who specialized in CP, explaining her medical history to him and asking what he would have recommended to do when she was younger.

The retired orthopedist wrote back: "Adult CP patients suffer little from joint disorders. . . . Intensive physiotherapy for two or three weeks, including swimming, can do wonders. The physiological compensation for disorders of motor control can bring considerable benefits. This is an adaptation to existing problems."

A new physical therapist confirmed what the Swiss orthopedist wrote. "Don't you see? The approach an institution takes depends on where it gets its funding. If you're funded by the Easter Seals Society, you take one approach. If you get funding from a medical school, you take another. If these places were not surgically oriented, they'd go out of business. With an adductor myotomy, they cut the muscle itself. It just weakens the leg. They don't do it to ambulatory people."

Since my last surgery in 1970, my left leg has grown three inches longer than my right leg. I now walk on the inner side of my right foot, which has grown increasingly callused. The inner lift of my shoe now needs repair after a few months' use. I tend to put this off for as long as possible so I am not stuck in the house without my shoes.

Did I make the right decision not to have surgery using the Ilizarov method that Dr. Frankel suggested? I've read that people who are disabled later in life do not harbor the same fear of surgery that people with congenital disabilities do. Is my decision a learned response, my giving in to the fear I learned by having numerous surgeries as a six-month-old infant and young child?

Or is it something else?

Paleontologist Owen Lovejoy writes: "For any quadruped to get up on its hind legs in order to run is an insane thing to do. It's plain ridiculous." And evolutionary theorist Emma Morgan, questioning the usual reasons given for the shift to bipedalism, notes that even Darwin, in *The Descent of Man,* took bipedalism for granted because the sequence of events seemed to go as follows: (1) our ancestral primates acquired greater dexterity and intelligence; (2) they learned to make tools and wield weapons, and it is easier to cope with these while standing upright with both arms free.

But later, in the twentieth century, fossils of our progenitors, including that of the famed hominid, "Lucy," show not even the slightest trace of evidence of tool making or weapon wielding. Morgan concludes that "the first bidepalists were not semihuman creatures. They were animals opting to walk on their hind legs. It was a costly option for them to take up, and we are still paying in instalments."

"Walking upright gives us the ability to carry food and babies, but it predisposes us to back problems," say Drs. Randolph M. Nesse and George C. Williams, authors of *Why We Get Sick.*

So, according to Morgan, as well as Nesse and Williams, back pain is the price paid by humans for evolution. Even if my lower body was symmetrical, back problems might have happened anyway simply because I am human.

And given the human propensity for back problems, who knows if, even after surgery, my back problems would cease. Morgan is right when she points out that an engineer confronted with the human body would surely start from scratch. The heart, lungs, kidneys, and other vital organs arranged symmetrically around a central spinal column would be the most viable option.

But, as Morgan reminds us, evolution doesn't work like that: "Every re-adaptation is a process of make-do and mend."

Emerald Buddha

The Emerald Buddha

A week before I travel to Thailand, I am surrounded by books on Thai culture. I am trying to discern how Thais will react and relate to my disability. One book cautions never to point your feet toward someone in Thailand. It is disrespectful to do so, even more so in a *wat*, a temple, where you should sit on the floor with your legs underneath you and to the side. How would I communicate that I intend no disrespect? Because I don't really have ankles, I can't do much about where my feet point, let alone tuck my feet neatly underneath me and to the side.

In Southeast Asia, disabled people are often hidden in the home, away from neighbors' eyes. What constitutes a disability in much of Asia also differs from what most people would consider a disability here in the States. A child born with clubfoot or a harelip, considered disabilities in many Asian cultures, is more likely to be given up for adoption in Bangkok than in New York City.

Eighty-five percent of Thais are Buddhists, and Buddhists believe in reincarnation. Physical disability is understood as a manifestation of having done something in a previous life that requires you to learn something through being disabled in this one. In Buddhist culture, most people think they will acquire merit in their next life when acting charitably not only toward monks but toward the disabled. However, some might regard disability as something evil, the disabled person as a demon, similar to the view of disability Western Judeo-Christian cultures inherited from the Middle Ages.

To the Hmong, who live among the hill tribes of northern Thailand and who also believe in reincarnation, giving birth to a disabled child is a sign that the parents did something in their previous or current lives, which caused the impairment. Yet to the Hmong, many impairments also lend a spiritual aura to those who have them. In Hmong culture, for example, people diagnosed with epilepsy often become shamans, performing rituals that bring together the seen and the unseen worlds.

On my first day in Bangkok, at Sanam Luang, I sit in an open, grassy-field park across from Wat Phrae Kaew, the most venerated temple in Thailand, which houses the revered Emerald Buddha. Awaiting me behind a large, white, fortress-sized wall is the *wat*'s ornate red and green roofs, as well as the large golden *chedi,* a conelike structure housing sacred ashes.

I enter the crowded palace grounds. This could be Disneyland.

I gaze at the temple buildings, watched over by *yaksha,* large statues of demonlike guards, pass statues of the mythical *kinaree,* half woman and half bird. Ethereal pinks, lavenders, yellows, maroons, and greens reflect off small shards of mirror bezeled into the temple walls. I notice one of the human guards plucking his nose hairs while looking at his reflection in front of the temple gate.

Before I enter the *wat,* an English sign tells me it is time to take off my shoes. I have fretted over this moment for six months. How will people react to my feet and to my limping into and around the temple with my cane? Am I even capable of walking around the temple without my shoes?

I sit down on a bench and remove my shoes. I leave them among all the others on the shelves, and think of all the shoes on the shelves of Frank's store on Harway Avenue.

Away from home, I am not used to being parted from my shoes, and I am more than a bit concerned. I know my shoes won't be mistaken for someone else's but can't stop worrying about what I would do, how I could continue my trip, let alone explain my situation, if they were somehow lost or stolen in Thailand.

Careful not to touch the large door lintel with my feet, another Thai custom I have learned from my reading, I enter the temple.

There are hundreds of silent worshippers inside. The walls are painted with frescoes depicting the life of the Buddha and the emperors. At a distance, I barely discern what all, Buddhist and tourist alike, have come to see: the small carved Buddha sitting in the madras lotus position, dressed in solid gold robes, high up on a succession of spectacularly gilded and canopied altars. Above its head are five golden umbrellas, positioned as halos, signifying the Buddha as most holy.

Shoeless, using my cane, I make my way down the side of the temple to a midway point where worshippers are seated on the floor. Am I the only *farang*, foreigner, in the temple? So far, everyone is too entranced by the Emerald Buddha to have noticed me.

I rest my cane on the floor and, leaning on my left hand, I manage to approximate the required position, legs underneath and to the right, a position I thought I couldn't assume. I notice two orange-robed monks in lotus position, each on a slightly raised platform to the left and right of the altar. The monks look straight ahead and a low chant seems to emanate from their throats.

Sitting on the floor, I stare at the Emerald Buddha, which begins to look like a blanket-clad infant, regal if slightly spoiled. I sense the power of its unflappable gaze. Size doesn't matter. Paying attention to its serene presence, I understand its allure.

I watch many worshippers, one by one, then in larger groups, move to the altar and, from their knees in one fluid motion, prostrate themselves in front of the Emerald Buddha. The younger monks, who sit on slightly raised platforms in the front of the altar, tie white strings to the wrists of the worshippers. I watch each prostrate worshipper flow to an upright position, then back away toward the door to the temple.

Soon, I realize one of my legs has fallen asleep, and I know I won't be able to hold my position on the floor, one leg underneath me, another to the side, much longer.

Outside, I retrieve my shoes that, thankfully, I find easily among the piles of others'. I readjust my eyes to the bright sun, take a swig of water from a bottle I took with me this morning, and, surprised that nobody seemed to notice me in the sacred temple, make my way out of the palace gates to the river.

Fifteen minutes later, I am taking the ferry across and up the river to Wat Mahathat, where I will visit the amulet market. From the boat, I watch the mongrel dogs sleeping on the piers, listen to the piercing whistle from the boy at the back, signaling how close or far the River Express is to the pier.

My map tells me Mahathat is the next stop. I position myself near the ferry's exit, and when I think we have maneuvered close enough to the pier I leap off the boat—

Only to be caught by two men, each holding one of my arms.

It takes me a moment to realize that the boat was too far from the pier and that I was falling forward, my cane landing with a crisp thud, newer wood on older wood, just as the men stopped me from my fall.

"Okay, I'm okay," I try to tell the two Thai men who stand next to me smiling broadly. I didn't see them before I jumped, and I'm still not sure where they came from. "*Khap krun khap, khap krun khap,*" I hear myself say, thanking the two men over and over, to show my appreciation, as well as assure myself I am okay.

My heart beats rapidly. I take a few moments on a bench to gather myself, inspecting my clothes to make sure I have not torn them, my limbs for scrapes. When the boy's by-now-familiar whistle from the back of the ferry calls my attention away from my still-shaking body, I look toward the end of the pier, expecting to see the ferry still at Mahathat and all eyes of all the passengers to be looking at me, the disabled *farang* who jumped off the ferry way too early.

But all I see are the murky green-brown waves of the Chao Phraya River lapping against the pier. The ferry boy's whistle comes from the next stop on the opposite riverbank. The two men who prevented me from being hurled into the churning muddy water have, as fast as their rescue, disappeared.

The Old Monk-Priest

Hundreds of miles from Bangkok is Chiang Mai, Thailand's northern capital and second largest city. Doi Suthep, the sacred mountain just outside of Chiang Mai, is home to Wat Prathat, Chiang Mai's most sacred temple. This late afternoon, however, my guide, Bun, drives me to what he calls "his temple" on the other side of Doi Suthep.

Chiang Mai reminds me of Santa Fe, New Mexico. Both are small cities once part of a different nation. Both were remote outposts surrounded by a different, sometimes hostile, culture. The indigenous hill tribe cultures around Chiang Mai and the pueblo cultures around Santa Fe produce highly coveted crafts. Both cities are growing very quickly, which threatens the unique culture that attracts so many visitors.

In Chiang Mai, concrete housing overwhelms the traditional teak dwellings. As in Bangkok, three-wheeled motorized *tuk-tuks* have all but supplanted the pedal-propelled *samlors*. Still, Chiang Mai, surrounded by the northern mountains and filled with wooden temples, retains its traditional culture.

Reaching the outskirts of the city, Bun drives us past factories. "Rice paddies used to be here," he tells me.

As we begin our drive up the other side of the mountain, skeletons of large hotels can be seen on the horizon, a demarcation of the new expansive city limits of Chiang Mai. Abandoned giant metal cranes abut steel skeletons. Due to overbuilding and the Asian financial crisis of the 1990s, progress has halted. The evolution of a city is at a standstill.

"What is going to happen to those buildings?" I ask Bun.

"Nobody knows. Money ran out. A good thing. Too many people here now. Changes the spirit of Chiang Mai. No more rice. No more hill tribes. No more mountains."

As we drive over a crest, Bun slows down the car. In front of us are many bulldozers leveling the land.

"What are they doing?" I ask.

"Condominiums."

"Who will live in them?"

"Nobody knows."

"The villagers?"

"Not the villagers. Villagers can't afford."

Bun drives a bit further and stops the car in front of a crumbling hutlike building. If I did not know that Bun's temple was our afternoon's destination, I would not think this building a temple. The collapse of the structure seems imminent.

"I won't be long," Bun tells me. "You come inside. You are welcome." I watch him open an almost unhinged door. He goes inside.

I am eager to see the temple because it is not on the itinerary for most of Bun's guests. But I also want to give Bun the time he needs alone with the monk-priest he has come to visit. I get out of the car and watch a tractor level the field in front of the temple.

I turn and walk toward the uneven door and open it.

Inside the temple it is dark. My sun-drenched eyes take a few minutes to adjust. I remain in the back of the temple, one unadorned room, not like the more extravagant temples I've seen throughout Thailand. This room is like the old, rarely used community room in my childhood Brooklyn apartment building. A few beamed columns hold up the roof. Unlike other temples, this one has only one Buddha statue on the raised altar. I see a few candles surrounding the lone white plaster figure, which is adorned with now-familiar yellow-sashed offerings.

In the corner of the altar, to the right of the Buddha, I notice a very old man lying on his side, right hand holding up his head, his position like that of the sleeping Buddhas I have seen in other temples. The old man is reclining on a mattress that looks quite lived in, so I assume it is his bed. He wears a burnt orange robe, not the bright saffron robes of most monks but the color of a dark autumn leaf. This old man is a high priest.

Monks have been present in many of the temples I have visited, but I have yet to see a high priest. In other temples, an occasional worshipper will come forward and a monk will tie a white string around the worshipper's wrist. Not once have I seen a monk and a worshipper engage in conversation inside a temple.

But here, in this temple, Bun, my guide, is standing in front of the reclining high priest. They seem to be engaged in a serious conversation. After a few minutes, Bun bows his head and appears to be receiving the monk's blessing. Then, he helps the elderly man to change his position. Now sitting upright, his legs folded beneath him, the monk's gravelly voice is stronger. It echoes through the temple.

The monk-priest speaks to Bun, but does not look at him. His gaze is directed above Bun's head, toward me at the back of the temple. The old monk-priest is blind. He holds Bun's hand. Before turning toward me, Bun gives the old man an envelope.

Back outside in the sun, I ask Bun about the envelope he gave to the monk.

"Money. The village supports him. He is their priest."

"But this isn't your village."

"He has been my family's priest since I was a young boy. When I was a monk, he was my teacher. Now he is old. He cannot see. He cannot hear good. It is my merit to give to him what he needs. He wasn't born blind."

Back in the car, we drive past now-dormant bulldozers. It is close to sunset as we head down the opposite side of Doi Suthep, the sacred mountain.

As we pass what used to be rice paddies, I ask Bun, "What's going to happen to the temple when the condominiums are built? If there are no villagers who will support the monk?"

No answer.

I have seen very few disabled people in Thailand. All but one were selling lottery tickets on the streets in Bangkok. The other was a blind beggar-musician, sitting against a wall playing an accordion-like instrument during a street festival in Kanchanaburi. But here, in the mountains just north of Chiang Mai, this blind monk-priest is being taken care of by those he served. Had he been born blind, could he have held such a revered role? How, then, would he have survived?

There is little light left in the sky. I see the outlines of the unfinished hotels on the outskirts of Chiang Mai.

"Maybe the building of the condominiums will stop, like these hotels," I offer.

"When you opened the door to the temple my monk knew you were *farang*," Bun tells me when we reach the stone walls of the old city of Chiang Mai. "He also told me: 'his legs do not make him lazy.'"

Extinct Like the Wolf and Tiger

"I could not have believed how wide was the difference, between savage and civilized man," Darwin wrote shortly after the *Beagle* arrived at Tierra del Fuego on December 17, 1832. In Tierra del Fuego, Captain FitzRoy planned to repatriate York Minster, Jemmy Button, and Fuegia Basket, the three Fuegians he had named and relocated to England on his previous journey to South America in 1828. FitzRoy believed the three Anglicized Fuegians could help establish a local Anglican mission, one of his goals for the *Beagle* expedition.

Anchoring off the coast of Tierra del Fuego, Darwin followed the tradition of his family's motto, found on the Darwins' heraldic coat of arms: *Cave et aude,* Watch and listen. He watched and listened to a "group of Fuegians partly concealed by the entangled forest . . . perched on a wild point overhanging the sea; and as we passed by, they sprang up, and waving their tattered cloaks sent forth a loud and sonorous shout. The savages followed the ship, and just before dark we saw their fire, and again heard their wild cry."

Darwin was interested in how the Fuegians reacted to Jemmy Button: "They immediately perceived the difference between him and the rest, and held much conversation between themselves on the subject. An old man addressed a long harangue to Jemmy, which it seems was to invite him to stay with him." But Jemmy Button could understand little of his native language and seemed ashamed of his countrymen, who marveled at the whiteness of Darwin's skin.

Even though it was the summer solstice, snow covered the hills. Darwin found the climate "wretched." The Fuegian wigwam, which "merely consists of a few broken branches stuck in the ground, and very imperfectly thatched on one side with a few tufts of grass and rushes," seemed to take only "the work of an hour." Darwin described the wigwam as offering "no more cover than the form of a hare," scarcely providing protection from the wind and rain. The Fuegians slept, five or six together, naked "on the wet ground coiled up like animals."

To Darwin, the Fuegians were some of the "most abject and miserable creatures" he had ever seen. The men of the central tribes wore "an otterskin, or some small scrap about as large as a pocket-handkerchief, which is barely sufficient to cover their backs as low down as their loins. It is laced across the breast by strings, and according as the wind blows, it is shifted from side to side." On board the *Beagle,* he encountered a woman "suckling a recently-born child," who "came one day alongside the vessel and remained there whilst sleet fell and thawed on her naked bosom, and on the skin of her naked child."

Darwin thought "these poor wretches stunted in growth, their hideous faces bedaubed with white paint, their skins filthy and greasy, their hair entangled, their voices discordant, their gestures violent and without dignity. Viewing such men, one can hardly make oneself believe they were fellow-creatures, and inhabitants of the same world."

Eventually, Jemmy Button, York Minster, and Fuegia Basket reacclimated to their tribe. Returning from an inland excursion, Darwin found the three Anglicized Fuegians shed of their Victorian dress and manners. He saw for the first time that culture was nothing more than a costume, acquired or lost in response to social context.

Like Darwin in Tierra del Fuego, Wallace, in the Amazon, encountered a culture very different from his own. There, he was accompanied by a group of natives while journeying to the Serra de Cobati, the prime nesting area for the white umbrella bird, around twelve miles through the forest from San Joaquim on the Vaupés River.

In the forest, Wallace's gun caught on overhanging branches, his shirts were spiked by the climbing plants, and his hat was constantly knocked off by the dense flora. The natives, however, "were all naked, or, if they had a shirt or trousers, carried them in a bundle on their heads." Wallace had no doubt he was looked upon "as a good illustration of the uselessness and bad consequences of wearing clothes on a forest journey." He let the native hunting party take the lead. By doing so, he moved beyond the trading and Christian culture of the great river systems, toward an indigenous way of life that he began to understand and appreciate on its own terms.

In 1854, in Borneo, Wallace likened the grace of the Dyaks to that of the finest Grecian statues in the British Museum. He noted his own modesty, his embarrassed reaction to the near-nakedness of the Dyaks, but also realized that in Borneo no such shame against the naked body had taken root. He found the impressive health and physical acumen of the Dyaks superior to his own. Later, in New Guinea, Wallace described each unclothed limb of the Papuans as made to be admired. He saw how these people were well adapted to their environment.

However, in his paper "The Development of Human Races under the Law of Natural Selection," Wallace wrote that, if colonization comes to New Guinea, there was little doubt that the Papuan race would become extinct. He could not imagine this energetic people would submit to slavery or domestic servitude. With the white man's advance, the Dyaks and Papuans would become extinct, like the islands' wolf and tiger.

Shoeless in Phang Nga Bay

How did I get here?

"My shoes brought me here," could be my answer.

But sitting alone in this narrow fiberglass kayak, looking out at the craggy limestone islands, monoliths more tall than wide, I am not wearing any shoes. My shoes, battered from trekking about in Thailand the past month, remain safely in the larger boat.

I watch a small fishing prow approach. The fishermen wave to me as the boat passes by. Do they wonder what I'm doing here, just before sunset, all alone in the middle of the bay?

As I row to Sunset Point, where I am supposed to meet my fellow travelers, I think how, although I made it up the seventiered Erawan waterfall last week, today I decided to forego a long hike up one of the limestone mountains. Instead, I spent the time paddling around Phang Nga Bay.

I know I have reached Sunset Point because I see the familiar boat, from which I kayaked hours ago, anchored in the bay. Reaching the boat, with assistance, on the arms of Joe and Piat, two Thai crewmen, I am lifted from my kayak to the iron rung ladder of the larger boat.

It is now long past dusk, and beneath me the surface of the bioluminescent water sparkles with each wave. On the top deck, I locate my shoes just where I left them. Shoes in hand, I climb down to the lower deck, go into the cabin, and gather what I will need for the night. I put my shoes in a Ziploc bag (I will need them to get around on the sandy beach) along with toothpaste, my toothbrush, and a small bottle of mouthwash. I seal the bag so what's inside will be safe from the water. Soon, Joe and Piat will help me again, this time down into a larger inflatable kayak, and they will row me and the four other tourists over to the beach where we will camp for the night.

Throughout my three days on the water, Joe and Piat, as well as the other Thai crew members, have instinctually known when I needed assistance and when I was okay doing something alone. Not once have they asked me whether I needed help. And not once have I had to ask for help. Whenever I needed assistance it was as if they could, in advance, read my mind.

Landing on the beach of a small limestone island in southern Thailand, I am once again helped off the boat, onto the shore.

Alone in my tent, I wonder how the old blind monk-priest knew I was disabled. I think about the two ferrymen who saved me from falling into the Chao Praya River in Bangkok. Did Joe and Piat, like the two ferrymen, simply observe and, by quietly paying attention, understand what I could do unassisted and what I might need help doing?

Was this because Buddhists view the body differently than we do in Western culture? After all, to Buddhists, living in a body is only a passing phase. I wonder how the two ferrymen knew I was going to jump ashore too soon. How long had they been watching me?

Departure From the Original Type

In 1857, while Darwin was at home in Downe considering the consequences of his developing theory, Wallace was still in the faraway Moluccas, the islands west of New Guinea, from where he sent his paper, "On the Natural History of the Aru Islands," to both Darwin and Lyell. Darwin responded:

> This summer will be the 20th year (!) since I opened my first notebook, on the question how & in what way do species & varieties differ from each other.— I am now preparing my work for publication, but I find the subject very large, that though I have written many chapters, I do not suppose I shall go to press for two years.—I have never heard how long you intend to stay in the Malay Archipelago; I wish I might profit by the publication of your Travels there before my work appears, for no doubt you will reap a large harvest of facts.—

After yet another bout with malaria, Wallace settled in Ternate in the Moluccas to write "On the Tendency of Varieties to Depart Indefinitely from the Original Type," which would become known as his Ternate paper. Still weak, living in a dilapidated hut in the jungle, he thought about what was close by. He focused his attention on the differences between the Malays and the Papuans. Were they two distinct races or variations of the same race?

Wallace became increasingly interested in how one species changed, slowly or rapidly, into another. He wanted to understand how, if one species gradually changed into another, there continued to be so many distinct species that differed from their nearest allies by slight yet perfectly definite traits.

Then, like Darwin, he remembered Malthus's "Principles of Population," which he had read twelve years before. He considered Malthus's "positive checks to increase"—disease, accidents, war, and famine—that keep down the population of races, more so among the so-called "savage races" than among the "civilised people." Then, it occurred to Wallace that these causes, or their equivalents, are continually acting in animals, as well. But animals generally breed much more rapidly than do humans. Since rapidly breeding animal populations do not regularly increase from year to year, the destruction every year from Malthus's "positive causes" must be enormous. Otherwise, Wallace deduced, the world long ago would have been populated with those species that breed most quickly.

"Why do some die and some live?" he asked. His answer was that, on the whole, the best fitted live: "From the effects of disease the most healthy escaped; from enemies, the strongest, the swiftest, or the most cunning; from famine, the best hunters or those with the best digestion; and so on." Wallace realized that this "self-acting" process would "*improve the race,* because in

every generation the inferior would inevitably be killed off and
the superior would remain—that is *the fittest would survive*."

But he went on to expand his idea that the fittest would
survive:

> Then at once I seemed to see the whole effect of this,
> that when changes of land and sea, of climate, or
> food supply, or of enemies occurred—and we know
> that such changes have always been taking place—
> in conjunction with the amount of individual vari-
> ation that my experience as a collector had shown
> me to exist, then all the changes necessary for the
> adaptation of the species to the changing conditions
> would be brought about; and as great changes in the
> environment are always slow, there would be ample
> time for the change to be effected by the survival of
> the fittest in every generation.

In this way, Wallace tied his ideas of survival of the fittest to
the changing environment in which a species lives.

Wallace sent his Ternate paper to Darwin on the mail boat
leaving the Moluccas on March 9, 1858. The paper reached
Darwin at Downe on either May or June 18, 1858; the record is
not clear.

After reading Wallace's paper, Darwin wrote to Lyell,
enclosing the paper as Wallace requested. Darwin noted that
he remembered how, a year or so before, Lyell had recommended to him another paper by Wallace. Years after having
dismissed that earlier paper as "more of the same," Darwin
now remarked that not only was Wallace's new paper worth
reading but he had never seen a more striking coincidence: if
Wallace had seen his 1842 manuscript sketch, he could not

have written a better short abstract of it. "Even his terms now stand as Heads of my Chapters," Darwin told Lyell.

Lyell, in consultation with botanist Joseph Hooker of the Royal Botanic Gardens, proposed that Darwin and Wallace should have their discoveries announced jointly at the Linnean Society. But Darwin, too distraught over his baby son Charles's scarlet fever, did not respond. Earlier, Darwin's older children had survived the same illness, but Charles, the youngest, died on June 28, 1858.

After his son's death, Darwin wrote to Lyell saying that he would be glad to publish a dozen-page sketch of his general views on evolution. Before Darwin received Wallace's Ternate paper, he had had no intention of publishing so soon. Now, he feared being preempted by Wallace was not a valid reason to publish. Darwin asked Lyell: "Do you not think that his having sent me this sketch ties my hands?"

On July 1, 1858, at the Linnean Society in London, unbeknownst to Wallace, extracts from Darwin's unpublished 1844 essay; a selection of Darwin's September 1857 letter to American naturalist Asa Gray, which included the principle of divergence; and Wallace's Ternate paper were read.

A Hole in a Shoe

When I was in college, when my shoes needed fixing, I mailed them, insured, to my parents, in a box prepared by my father, who at the time worked as manager of the shipping department of a women's sportswear firm in Manhattan. On my mother's way to work as secretary at a local elementary school, she dropped off my shoes at Frank's, the cobbler. Never longer than a week and a half later, my father mailed back my newly resoled, repatched, and polished shoes. I kept the box until a few months later, when I once again packed my shoes inside to send them for repair.

Over the years I learned to care for my shoes, setting them out on old newspaper and polishing them. I shined my shoes until they gleamed. After spending half an hour rubbing them with a rag dabbed with brown shoe polish, I left them on my desk overnight to dry, and in the morning they looked like they had when I first wore them, or when they came back to me from the shoemaker wrapped neatly in my father's specially prepared box.

Now, I send my shoes to Frank on my own. For five years, he has been telling me I need a new pair of shoes. "Your shoes will not hold up much longer," he warned me after repairing the hole in my shoe after my trip up the Beehive. Could it be my worn shoes, not adapted for the way my feet have changed, are causing the pain I've been feeling in my right knee?

I search the Yellow Pages under "Orthopedic Appliances" to find a local orthotics lab.

"For us to make you shoes, we'll need a prescription from your doctor," the secretary says.

A prescription? If I walked into the lab it would be obvious I need the shoes.

"For the insurance," the secretary tells me.

I call Dr. Frankel's office and, two weeks later, I receive a letter from the now sixty-five-year-old Dr. Frankel: "Kenny Fries cannot ambulate without orthopedic shoes." Prescription in hand, for the first time in seventeen years I go to be fitted for a new pair of shoes.

The Orthotics and Prosthetics Lab is in a small strip mall a few miles from where I live. The lab is a storefront divided into a waiting room with metal folding chairs, a smaller cubicle serving as an office, and an even smaller, fluorescently lit examination room with the familiar paper-clad examination table against the wall.

In the examination room, Jim, the orthoticist, clad in his white lab coat, looks intently through his thick black-rimmed glasses. Before he puts plastic bags over my feet, he puts two thin strips of soft material down the center of each foot and lower leg. This slow-moving, ever-smiling, chubby man who looks like a model young husband and father makes a mold of my feet, not with plaster but with fiberglass. "You'll be amazed at how light your new shoes will be. We use new materials since these were made," Jim says, holding my worn old pair for a closer inspection.

"I miss the heat from the plaster."

But when Jim reaches into a drawer and pulls out the same kind of saw Jerry Miller used to cut plaster, I begin to sweat.

"You still need that?" I ask, wincing.

"Some things don't change," he answers.

"What's to protect my leg?"

"The two strips of resistant material underneath."

I jump.

"Stay still or you won't be needing any shoes at all," Jim says without looking up from the blade.

When Jim slips the molds from my feet, I am surprised when the fiberglass doesn't pull my leg hairs. "That's what the plastic bag is for."

Three weeks later, back at the orthotics lab, I look at my new, slightly lighter shade of brown shoes. They don't look as if they will hold up for fifteen weeks, let alone fifteen years.

"The lift has been put on my left shoe, not the right," I say.

"You're kidding," Jim says as he opens my file to check his notes. "My mistake," he says sheepishly as he reads "three-inch lift on left shoe" from a page in his manila folder. "Give me another week."

When I try on the newly relifted shoes, for a moment I feel as though I'm wearing my first pair of Eneslow shoes, over thirty years ago. The new material is so soft. Lifting my right shoe no longer feels as if I am weightlifting. I imagine Cinderella dancing with Prince Charming across the office floor.

But midnight comes too early. As I continue walking from exam room to waiting room and back again, my right foot begins to feel precarious, as if I am walking on high heels. As I plant the right shoe on the floor, all of a sudden I stumble. My foot takes a quick dip to the inside, almost rolling over, twisting my fragile right knee.

Jim compares my new shoes to the old shoes. "I knew this wasn't going to be easy the moment you walked in the door."

"Why not make a pair just like the ones I've been wearing, only with the newfangled materials?" I offer.

"You'd be without your shoes for at least four weeks."

"Would they come back in good shape?" I ask. Thoughts of anonymous shoemakers somewhere in Buffalo pouring plaster into the shoes I've worn for all these years makes me more than a little anxious.

"As a last resort, we might have to take that chance," he says. "I wanted to make a new pair for the way your body is now. That would be best for the long term, but that might not be possible."

Long term? My old shoes have lasted for close to two decades. Obviously, my bones, my muscles, and my neurological system have learned and adapted to the way I've been walking for so long. Rewiring this body for a new way of walking will not be easy.

The Hidden Bond of Connection

After their joint presentation at the Linnean Society, Darwin realized that Wallace was more than a supplier of species needed for his research. As his friend Hooker prepared the papers for publication in the society's *Journal,* Darwin knew he had to tell Wallace, still halfway across the world, what had transpired. He wrote to Lyell: "I do not think that Wallace can think my conduct unfair, in allowing you & Hooker to do whatever you thought fair. My plans for publication are all changed."

Darwin enlisted Hooker, who had helped arrange the Linnean Society presentation, to write to Wallace about the proceedings, along with the edited presentation as printed in the *Journal.* Enclosed with Hooker's note, Darwin enclosed a letter of his own.

Four months later in New Guinea, Wallace, returning from another expedition in search of birds of paradise and recuperating from yet another bout of malaria, received the letters from England. He wrote to both Hooker and Darwin, but only his letter to Hooker survives:

It would have caused me much pain & regret had Mr. Darwin's excess of generosity led him to make public my paper unaccompanied by his own much earlier & I doubt not much more complete views on the same subject. I must again thank you for the course you have adopted, which while quite strictly just to both parties, is so favourable to myself.

Writing to his mother, Wallace confided, "This insures me the acquaintance of these eminent men on my return home."

In the summer of 1858, Darwin took his family to the Isle of Wight, away from the scarlet fever epidemic in Downe. Buoyed by the change of scenery, pride in his son William's scholarship to attend Christ's College in Cambridge, and prodded by Hooker's request for another article for the *Journal,* he turned his attention to elaborating his theory. Returning home in mid-August, shut up in his study surrounded by decades of research, Darwin continued writing beyond "the sketch" he had promised Hooker. In October, he wrote to Hooker: "You cannot imagine what a service you have done me in making me make this abstract, for though I thought I had got all clear, it has clarified my brains much, by making me weigh relative importance of the several elements."

That autumn, the Linnean papers were reprinted in many popular natural history magazines. Letters were written; reviews were published. Upon reading the papers, Cambridge professor Alfred Newton wrote:

Never shall I forget the impression it made upon me. Herein was contained a perfectly simple solution of all the difficulties which had been troubling me for months past. . . . it came to me like the direct

revelation of a higher power; and I awoke the next
morning with the consciousness that there was an
end of all the mystery in the simple phrase, 'Natural
Selection.'

The death of his sister Marianne, the illness of his daughter,
Henrietta, and incessant work began to affect Darwin. He
began to suffer from dyspepsia, extreme stomach pain, and his
doctors recommended numerous rest and water cures.

Darwin persevered and, finally, in May 1859, he finished his
manuscript. He consulted Lyell about publishers and settled on
Lyell's own, John Murray, which had earlier issued the second
edition of Darwin's *Journals of Researches*.

The new, not-yet-titled book began with a discussion of the
variation of organisms, using Darwin's years of work on barnacles, primroses, and wild horses. Then came the analogy
between domestic selection—how breeders of plants and animals
selected for certain traits—and natural selection in the wild. He
supported his theory by invoking Malthus: given the limitations of food and space, more individuals are born than can survive and reproduce. "It is the doctrine of Malthus applied with
manifold force to the whole animal and vegetable kingdoms, for
in this case there can be no artificial increase of food, and no
prudential restraint from marriage."

Darwin described the struggle in nature:

It may be said that natural selection is daily and
hourly scrutinising, throughout the world, every
variation, even the slightest; rejecting that which is
bad, preserving and adding up all that is good;
silently and insensibly working, whenever and
wherever opportunity offers, at the improvement of

each organic being in relation to its organic and inorganic conditions of life.

The abundant evidence he supplied fell into four categories: biogeography, paleontology, embryology, and morphology. In his section on biogeography, the study of the geographical distribution of species, Darwin wrote about the clustering pattern of "closely allied species": very similar forms of mockingbirds he found on different islands in the Galápagos; two rheas, two similar species of flightless birds, *Rhea americana* and *Pterocnemia pennata,* which occupied adjacent areas of South America; and small rodents in South America, two found in the drylands and two in the wetlands.

Paleontology, the study of extinct species in fossils, revealed a similar clustering pattern over epochs of time. As an example, Darwin used the North American horselike species known as *Hyracotherium,* which was succeeded by *Orohippus,* followed by *Epihippus,* then *Mesohippus,* in succeeding layers of geological strata.

Embryology looks at the developmental stages embryos pass through before birth. For example, embryos of mammals pass through stages during which they resemble the embryos of reptiles. To Darwin, "The embryo is the animal in its less modified state." This state "reveals the structure of its progenitor."

Morphology, the science of anatomical shape and design, was described by Darwin as the "very soul" of natural history. The five-digit skeletal structure of the vertebrate hand, for example, can be found not only in humans but in apes, raccoons, bears and, with modified structures, in cats, bats, porpoises, lizards, and turtles. Vestigial structures, like the human appendix or the basic hind legs in snakes, also provide morphological evidence of natural selection.

Darwin showed how his theory explained the most intractable questions of nineteenth-century biology, "descent being . . . the hidden bond of connexion which naturalists have been seeking." He explained how natural selection, rather than some divine plan, explained the anatomical resemblances of species, and how "descent" explained vestigial organs, remnants of anatomical history.

He struggled to find the right words. He admitted to Lyell that he did not intend to portray natural selection as an intentional process. Darwin tried using "natural preservation" but stuck with "natural selection." For a while, he settled on "contrivance" instead of "adaptation." He called the entire process "descent with modification," avoiding "evolution." And he never used what would become the most famous phrase of all, "survival of the fittest," which was later coined by philosopher Herbert Spencer in 1864.

By comparing domesticated species with those in the wild, Darwin differentiated himself from Wallace. He also looked at species replacement by individual changes, rather than by groups of differences, the method described in Wallace's Ternate paper.

Expecting challenges to his theory, Darwin included admissions of the difficulties that some might encounter, including the gap in the fossil record and sterility between closely related species. He admitted to his readers: "I have felt the difficulty far too keenly to be surprised at any degree of hesitation in extending the principle of natural selection to such great lengths." Notably, to assuage religious readers, he omitted discussing the first origin of life, the origin of humans, and talk of God.

Darwin felt rushed. He deemed his 490-page book merely an "abstract" with abbreviated evidence, without footnotes or any list of sources. By the end of May 1858, his stomach ills increased. He began vomiting. He handed his manuscript to John Murray, his publisher, as well as to Hooker and Lyell, for review, and to female family members, including Emma and his daughter, Henrietta, for editing.

"I am becoming as weak as a child, miserably unwell & shattered," Darwin told Hooker as publication approached. In September 1859 he wrote to Hooker: "I have been so weary & exhausted of late. I have for months doubted whether I have not been throwing away time & labour for nothing." To his cousin, William Darwin Fox, he admitted, "My abominable volume . . . has cost me so much labour that I almost hate it."

"I am foolishly anxious for your verdict," he wrote to Lyell, who eventually told Darwin his book would throw "a flood of light on many classes of phenomena connected with the affinities, geographical distribution, and geological succession of organic beings, for which no other hypothesis has been able, or has even attempted to account." Darwin responded to Lyell's praise: "Now, I care not what the universal world says. . . . You would laugh if you knew how often I have read your paragraph, & it has acted like a little dram."

In November 1859, twenty-three years after he returned from his *Beagle* voyage, Darwin, aged fifty, published *On the Origin of Species*.

Lansman's Pool

Dark Water

Shoeless, I run to the Lansman's pool.

During the week, the fathers working in the city, the children busy all day at camp, the bungalow colony was a society of mothers. And on all sunny days the mothers could be found lounging by the pool. Some of the mothers swam; others played canasta or mah-jongg under an umbrella. These were the days before the ultraviolet rays of the sun were known to cause skin cancer; and my mother, unfamiliar with melanoma, enjoyed baking in the sun more than most.

After she served my brother and me lunch and sent us back to camp for the afternoon, my mother and her friends, dressed in variously solid-colored one-piece bathing suits, made their way in a procession to the pool. On the lawn of the small hill in the fenced-in pool area (never on the concrete surrounding the pool or on the gray-painted wood deck opposite the lawn) the mothers lay on their chaise longues, occasionally taking a dip in the shallow end of the pool.

Twice a day, at eleven in the morning and four in the

afternoon, the entire day camp assembled at the pool for "General Swim." We were sent home fifteen minutes before the appointed hour to change into our bathing suits. Then we gathered outside the pool fence, under our counselors' supervision. Anyone who was late was not allowed into the pool for the first fifteen minutes of General Swim.

Many of the mothers stayed on the lawn watching their children frolic in and out of the pool. But by the time four thirty came, most had packed up their lounge chairs, towels, and mahjongg sets, and headed home to begin preparations for dinner.

The pool itself was painted aquatic blue. Across the width of the pool was a buoyed rope that divided the water into shallow and deep sections. In the shallow end were two rows of silver bars that, along with the most shallow edge of the pool wall, created a kiddie corral for the youngest swimmers. In the deep end, at three-quarters the length of the pool, were two large blocks, one on each side, flat on top, angled on the side facing in, which created a place to sit, as well as a way to slide into the pool.

When I asked my mother why these blocks were built, she said they held the pool in place. Apparently, someone had thrown a firecracker into the pool, although some believed the pool had somehow frozen during winter and the Lansmans did not want to pay to build an entirely new pool so, to keep the pool intact, installed these blocks instead. Past the blocks, on each side of the pool, were two ladders, silver like the bars of the corral, and, at the deepest point, a diving board with minimum spring.

During General Swim only those who had passed the camp's deep water test were allowed past the rope into the deeper end of the pool. Only the oldest three groups in the camp were allowed to take the deep water test, which consisted of swimming four widths of the pool, from block to block, and treading water in the deep end for five minutes.

Everyone in the pool, no matter if swimming in front of or beyond the rope, had to have a buddy. When Mike, the lifeguard who also served as swim instructor for the camp, first blew his whistle, the mothers had to vacate the pool. Then, on his next whistle, the entire camp went screaming in. The next time the whistle blew, everyone, whether in the pool or out, had to be silent; those in the pool had to hold up high their buddy's hand. If you were caught without your buddy, you were docked and not allowed in the pool for the rest of General Swim.

At a quarter to five, when Mike the lifeguard blew the whistle, those campers from off-colony had to get out of the pool and make their way to the camp cars in front of the casino, which drove them home. At five minutes to five, Mike blew the whistle one more time and all campers had to leave the pool. Another day of camp had ended.

On especially hot days, Mike gave the pool key to an older counselor who kept the pool open an hour after camp. With most of the other kids gone, this was my favorite time to swim. After five in the afternoon, the pool water took on a darker hue. Of course this was because the light in the sky, especially during late afternoon in August, had begun to dim. But to me the dark blue water signified something other than the reflection of twilight in a swimming pool.

I have to remind myself that, during those summers in the pool at Lansman's, of all the hundreds of children in the camp, except for Marty Hirsch who had impaired vision, I was the only disabled child. With three toes on each foot, with scars and holes where pins were inserted during my operations, my physical difference, though always apparent, especially as I grew older and my peers grew taller faster than I, was more evident when I was wearing a swimsuit at the pool.

When did I start noticing other kids' curious or frightened stares? Was anybody else, my family or friends, aware of these stares? And why, even when I did realize how different my body was from the bodies of other boys, did I never recoil from exposing my naked legs at the pool, when I could have easily done so?

A New Science

"Many clouds upon our vision are of our own making," writes paleontologist Stephen Jay Gould, listing our "social and cultural biases, psychological preferences, and mental limitations (in universal modes of thought, not just individualized stupidity)" as causes for not accepting new ways of seeing and understanding the world. Gould warns that "The human contribution to this equation of difficulty becomes ever greater as the subject under investigation comes closer to the heart of our practical and physical concerns."

What could be closer to the heart of the practical and physical concerns of Victorian society than what Darwin proposed in *On the Origin of Species*?

Upon its publication, Darwin sent Wallace, still hunting for more birds of paradise in Ternate, a copy of the book, along with a note: "I hope there will be some little new to you, but I fear not much." In May 1860, Darwin received a response from Wallace, but that letter has been lost.

Wallace told George Silk, an old school friend, he had read the book "five or six times, each time with increasing admiration. It will live as long as the 'Principia' of Newton. . . . Mr. Darwin has given the world a new science, and his name should, in my opinion, stand above that of every philosopher of ancient and modern times." To naturalist Charles Bates, Wallace admitted, "I do not honestly believe that with however much patience I had worked and experimented on the subject, I could never have approached the completeness of his book, its vast accumulation of evidence, and its admirable tone and spirit. I really feel thankful that it has not been left to me to give the theory to the world."

Darwin's May 18, 1860, letter told Wallace:

> Your letter pleased me very much, & I most completely agree with you on the parts which are strongest & which are the weakest. . . . Before telling you about the progress of opinion on subject, you must let me say how I admire the generous manner in which you speak of my book: most persons would in your position have felt some envy or jealousy. How nobly free you seem to be of this common feeling of mankind—But you speak far too modestly of yourself,—you would, if you had had my leisure, done the work just as well, perhaps better, than I have done it. . . . I can very plainly see as I lately told Hooker, that my Book would have been & be a flash in the pan, were it not for you, Hooker and a few others.

Darwin kept Wallace apprised of the reaction to natural selection. Lyell, Hooker, and anthropologist T. H. Huxley formed the most ardent support. Most geologists and naturalists tended to follow suit. Soon, Darwin's book was translated and published in editions in Germany, France, Italy, and Russia.

But attacks, some vitriolic and personal, were voiced: influential paleontologist Richard Owen ("If I must criticise, I shd. say, we do not want to know what Darwin believes & is convinced of, but what he can prove."); geologist Adam Sedgwick, Darwin's former Cambridge professor ("Parts of it I admired greatly; parts I laughed until my sides were sore; other parts I read with absolute sorrow; because I think them utterly false & grievously mischievous—You have *deserted*—after a start in that tram-road of all solid physical truth—the true method of induction—& started up a machinery as wild, I think, as Bishop Wilkin's locomotive that was to sail us to the moon"); and Samuel Wilberforce, bishop of Oxford ("Now we must say at once and openly . . . that such a notion is absolutely incompatible not only with single expressions in the word of God but with the whole representation of that moral and spiritual condition of man which is its proper subject matter.").

In January 1861, Wallace left Ternate for Timor, to fill some gaps in his collection. He collected some rare butterflies. In letters, he never wavered in his admiration of Darwin's book. Only years later did he confide to his doctor that when he first read *On the Origin of Species,* he put aside his own projected book. He would have to find another purpose for his notes and journals.

In his letters home, Wallace confessed his health was declining. He was exhausted and no longer able to withstand the privations of island jungle life. As he began planning to return to England, he wanted, more and more, to bring live birds of paradise home with him. Not only did he wish to eradicate the memory of the loss of his live collection in the Amazon, but he also thought the birds of paradise might provide him with financial security.

In April 1862, when Wallace returned to England, he was accompanied by two young male birds of paradise.

Something About You Kids

How did I learn about fear and shame?

Somehow, I know the answer to these questions lies in an episode that, to this day, my mother either cannot fully remember or, if she does remember, refuses to tell me what she remembers. Twenty-nine years later, I ask my mother why she had a fight with Isabel Levine.

"I don't know. It was something about you kids. I don't remember," is her reluctant reply. "Why do you want to know?"

The Levines were a family of four who lived at 1935 Shore Parkway, the apartment building across from ours at 2630 Cropsey Avenue. A few years after we began spending summers at Lansman's, the Levines began to summer at Lansman's, as well.

Sometime toward the middle of that summer, I remember my mother surrounded by two of her friends as they accompanied her back to our bungalow from the pool. I see my mother's dark tan skin, a striking contrast to her white one-piece bathing suit. I see my mother wearing her dark sunglasses, which I always thought too large for her face. I see my mother come into our bungalow and hear her bellow in an unfamiliar contralto, a voice deeper than her usual voice, a voice both clear and guttural: "How dare she say that to me. How dare she."

Somehow I know that the pain expressed in my mother's voice is because of something Isabel Levine said to her that afternoon at the pool. Somehow I know that what Isabel Levine said to my mother had to do with me. Somehow I know that when my mother enters our bungalow it is late afternoon and I am in the bedroom, still dressed in my bathing suit, stunned, not moving on my lower bunk bed, draped in a towel. A few minutes ago, I know I ran from the pool after hearing Isabel Levine say something to my mother about allowing me to run around the pool showing off my scars.

Something about you kids. Had Isabel's son Jeffrey, who was my age and in my group at camp, said something to me that I told my mother that day at the pool? Had my mother then confronted Isabel in front of their mutual friends? Or had Jeffrey told his mother how he felt about my legs, and had Isabel confronted my mother with Jeffrey's discomfort that afternoon?

Born in 1936 in the East New York section of Brooklyn, the second child and first daughter of Harry and Sally Nathanson, two assimilated born-in-the-States Jews, my mother, Joan, graduated, like many teenage girls at the time, from a commercial course in high school. Upon graduation and until the age of nineteen, when she married my father, Donald, she worked as a secretary at a small company in Manhattan. She gave birth to my brother, Stephen, in 1957. Nothing in her experience prior to my birth, three and a half years later, prepared her to raise a child with a disability. In 1960, years before there was a disability rights movement, disability was seen solely as a medical issue. It was over a decade before disability, spurred on by the growing disability rights movements, as well as the field of disability studies, would be viewed from a civil rights or cultural perspective.

My mother never found a reason for my impairment. Neither have I. But she was, somehow, at some point, able to let it go.

I still hear my mother's voice, somewhere between a threat and a wail. Even now, it is as if the tone of my mother's voice—its pain and its pride—is the closest I can get to the feelings of fear and shame I did not express as a boy. It is the closest I can get to knowing how much my mother loved and was proud of me when I was a child. And knowing this I also know our missed opportunity, hers as well as my own, to begin to untangle the still unexpressed feelings surrounding the situation we found ourselves in as I grew up.

Now, I remember those long-ago half-hours before dinner, after a full day's activity when I swam or floated on my back in the Lansman's pool, and I understand the dark blue color of the pool water in late afternoon. It is as if time—all the intervening years—is suspended, and the color of the water is the color of my mother's voice as she is led by her friends that sun-drenched afternoon, from the pool into the bungalow, with all of the summer gear stored inside, a bungalow that long ago burnt to the ground.

As I swim from block to block the short width of the pool, how quickly the dark water that keeps me afloat turns into that lower bunk bed where a part of me, and my relationship with my mother, remains as inert as those concrete blocks installed to keep intact and not have to build an entirely new pool.

Zoological Society of London

Metaphors

Back in England, Wallace unpacked his boxes, including his three thousand bird skins, twenty thousand beetles, shells, and some mammals. He arranged and annotated collections and drafted papers for the Zoological and Linnean societies, but delayed writing a book about his Malaysian journeys until he could study his collections in more detail.

The display of his birds of paradise at the Zoological Society, the first birds of paradise seen in England, received much attention, including such distinguished visitors as the Duke of Argyll. On May 27, 1862, Wallace spoke of his expeditions in search of the rare birds at the society, where he had been elected a fellow.

Despite all this activity, Wallace was not well and spent many days resting in his room at his sister and brother-in-law's house in Paddington. In mid-May, he was bedridden for ten days with a bad case of boils. "How puzzled you must be to know what to begin at," Darwin wrote to him, after inviting him to visit at Downe. Because of his health, Wallace had to decline the invitation. He sent Darwin a wild honeycomb from Timor, still full of honey, in his stead.

Wallace had a difficult time adjusting to the fast pace, noise, and grit of Victorian London. He used his recuperation to catch up on reading, including Darwin's book on orchids and published reactions to *On the Origins of Species*. He told Darwin that it seemed "you have assisted those who want to criticise you by your overstating the difficulties & objections—Several of them quote your own words as the strongest arguments against you."

Soon, business details and family obligations distracted Wallace from his work. He needed to sell his most recent collections. He had made a costly financial error when he helped finance the expansion of his brother-in-law's photographic firm. The collapse of the business necessitated Wallace's payment of his sister and brother-in-law's rent and debts, as well as loans to his mother. His years of independence and self-sufficiency in the jungle had come to an end.

Wallace finally met Darwin at Downe in June or July of 1862. The only record that the meeting took place is Wallace's mention of the visit in *My Life*, published in 1905. This meeting was the kind of scientific exchange that Wallace longed for, now that he was trying to make a life for himself in London. But scarlet fever cut his stay short. This time, it was Darwin's son, Leonard, and Emma who became ill. Soon after his stay at Downe, Wallace contracted pleurisy.

Criticism of Darwin's metaphor of natural selection persisted. "People will not understand that all such phrases are metaphors," Wallace told him. "I wish therefore to suggest to you the possibility of entirely avoiding this source of misconception in your great work . . . and I think it may be done without difficulty & very effectually by adopting Spencer's term . . . 'Survival of the fittest.'" Wallace explained that "This term is the plain expression of fact, natural selection is a metaphorical expression of it, and to a certain indirect sense, even personifying Nature, she does not so much select special various species as exterminate the most unfavourable ones." Wallace went through his copy of *Origin,* and crossed out "natural selection," replacing it with "survival of the fittest."

While preparing the fifth edition of *On the Origin of Species,* Darwin used the term "survival of the fittest" for the first time.

Shoes on Fire

According to the enclosed instructions, I am supposed to wear the new shoes for an hour the first day, two hours the next, and so on, until I am able to wear them comfortably for an entire day. For the next three weeks, once a week, I go to see Jim and he tinkers some more on my new-for-the-way-my-body-is-now shoes.

But after a week, I begin to feel a twinge in my right knee. Afraid to put my entire weight on my right leg, I compensate with my left. My back begins to ache. A muscle around my left hip begins to spasm. I feel vertigo. My spine, just below my neck, is sore. My head begins to pound.

By the third week, Jim decides to copy the flare, the slight indented curve, on my right shoe's inner edge that Frank instinctively knew to build into the lift. As I walk around Jim's office, the flare seems to do the job. Excited, I bring my new shoes home for what I hope will be, except for necessary maintenance, the last time. Thoughts of my new shoes begin to replace thoughts of the Ilizarov contraption.

But for the next three days, even with a new flare, after a full day of wearing my shoes, my right knee, hip, lower back, and neck hurt so much that I have difficulty sleeping.

"What should we do?" I ask Jim.

"It's your call," Jim answers. "I can remold your feet and this time send the new molds along with your old shoes and see what the factory can come up with or—"

"Or I could wear the new shoes and see if it gets better, over time." I look down at my new shoes, then at Jim, then back down at my shoes.

"I just don't want to do any damage to my body," I say.

I continue to wear my new shoes for two weeks, and the pain in my right knee, left hip, lower back, and neck continues. I begin to feel as I did before I visited Dr. Frankel, got my cane, and had my right shoe lifted to make my two legs the same length.

Convinced the pain can't keep getting worse, I take long, hot baths, and swallow eight Tylenols a day while wondering about the damage they will do to my liver.

I begin to forget appointments. I can't remember my own phone number. I am lethargic, depressed. I remain in bed until two in the afternoon, mourning the loss of the mobility I've had for thirty-seven years.

I stay awake thinking of when I was in the third grade, when my shoes were left for repair at Frank's. My father had dreamed the shoemaker's store was on fire. The whole store and all the shoes inside it—including mine—ablaze, sending clouds of gray smoke over our entire neighborhood. Soon, our entire apartment building, all sixteen stories of it, engulfed in the haze.

I think how everybody else is able to drive to the nearest mall and buy a new pair of shoes, put them on, and be on their way. I realize this line of thought will never get me anywhere but into a surgeon's office. The next day, I put the new shoes back on. I pack up my old shoes and deliver them to Jim. If the people making my new shoes have my old shoes, hopefully, they will have all the information they need to make me a new pair just like them.

"Give me four weeks," Jim tells me.

For four weeks, with my shoes somewhere in Buffalo, I have only the new shoes to wear. Fifteen minutes after putting them on, my right knee and back cause me to forget what I went into town to do. I spend most of the four weeks in my bed reading newspapers and magazines cover to cover.

baboon

Under the Form of the Baboon

In April 1866, Wallace, forty-three, married twenty-year-old Annie Mitten. Their son, Herbert Spencer Wallace, known as Bertie, was born in June 1867. During the 1860s, Wallace became increasingly interested and active in Spiritualism, attending séances ever since a medium had tapped out a message from his dead brother, Herbert.

By the late 1860s, both Darwin and Wallace had moved on to the subject of man. Wallace, in the closing paragraphs of *The Malay Archipelago,* dedicated to Darwin and published in 1869, echoed his 1864 paper, "The Development of the Human Races under the Law of Natural Selection." He said that despite European culture's progress in physical science and its applications, the European social and moral state remains barbaric. Wallace felt that European culture was a failure because of "our neglect to train and develop more thoroughly the sympathetic feelings and moral faculties of our nature." This, Wallace concluded, is what he learned from living among and observing "uncivilised man" in South America and the Spice Islands.

Wallace's first extended foray into the area of natural selection concerning man was a 1869 review in the *Quarterly* of new editions of Lyell's *Principles of Geology* and *Elements of Geology*. Before the review's publication, Wallace wrote to Darwin: "I venture for the first time on some limitation to the power of natural selection." Darwin responded that he was "intensely curious" to read Wallace's article, but hoped "you have not murdered too completely your own and my child."

In his review, Wallace wrote that natural selection and evolution

> may teach us how, by chemical, electrical, or higher natural laws, the organised body can be built up, can grow, can reproduce its like; but those laws and that growth cannot even be conceived as endowing the newly arranged atoms with consciousness. But the moral and higher intellectual nature of man is a unique phenomenon as was conscious life on its first appearance in the world, and the one is almost as difficult to conceive as originating by any law of evolution as the other.

Wallace suggested the human brain, the organs of speech, the hand, and the external form of man could not be explained by either variation or survival of the fittest. To him, the human brain was more powerful than was necessary for survival. Natural selection, he argued, improved an organ only through its adaptation to the pressure of environment. In the review's closing paragraphs he reiterated his firm belief in the laws of natural selection, but that in the development of man there seemed to be a "Power which has guided the action of those laws in definite directions and for special ends." He used the analogy that just as man intervened to develop the Guernsey milk cow or the London dray horse, "in the development of the human race, a Higher Intelligence has guided the same laws for nobler ends." He defined these "special ends" as "the infinite advancement of our mental and moral nature."

Darwin, in his copy of the *Quarterly* that contained Wallace's review, wrote "No" by this passage. He underlined his reaction three times, and wrote to Wallace: "I differ grievously from you and I am sorry for it. I can see no necessity for calling in an additional and proximate cause in regard to Man." Darwin did not accept any "miraculous additions at any one stage" in the development of man.

Darwin, during this time, was writing *The Descent of Man,* bringing together all he had learned to explain human ancestry. As early as 1838, in one of his notebooks, he had written: "Our descent, then, is the origin of our evil passions!—The devil under form of Baboon is our grandfather."

In July 1870, as he tackled a subject that many thought was not an area for science to study, Darwin once again felt ill. "Everything has been of late at a stand still with me," he told Hooker. "With respect to my own book, the subject grows so, that I really cannot say when I shall go to press." In November, he wrote to Wallace about his new book: "I much fear will quite kill me in your estimation."

Despite his ill health and other concerns, Darwin continued writing about his belief that

> Man still bears in his bodily frame the indelible stamps of his lowly origin. The early progenitors of Man were no doubt once covered with hair, both sexes having beards; their ears were pointed and capable of movement; and their bodies were provided

with a tail, having the proper muscles. . . . The foot, judging from the condition of the great toe in the foetus, was then prehensile; and our progenitors, no doubt, were arboreal in their habits, frequenting some warm, forest-clad spot. The males were provided with great canine teeth, which served them as formidable weapons.

He did not stop with the form of man. At the start of *The Descent of Man* he wrote that there is "no fundamental difference between man and the higher mammals in their mental faculties." He used examples of horses finding their way home, ants defending their property, chimpanzees using implements, and bower-birds' admiring their nests.

Darwin believed that speech evolved from the social vocalizations of apes:

As monkeys certainly understand much that is said to them by man, and as in a state of nature they utter signal-cries of danger to their fellows, it does not appear altogether incredible, that some unusually wise ape-like animal should have thought of imitating the growl of a beast of prey, so as to indicate to his fellow monkeys the nature of the expected danger. And this would have been a first step in the formation of language.

Central to *The Descent of Man* was Darwin's belief that sexual selection was "the most powerful means of changing the races of man." Darwin believed that characteristics in human beings, like in animals, were sustained and developed only because they related to reproductive success. In man, the development of traits not related to adaptation and survival but to reproductive success is similar to the development of peacocks' tail feathers to attract mates. Darwin mentioned skin color and hair texture as such characteristics.

Sexual selection also encompassed such emotional characteristics in humans as maternal love, bravery, altruism, obedience, and diligence. Social cohesion also came under the sexual selection rubric. "Sexual selection has been a tremendous job," Darwin told Wallace, who did not agree with his tenets of sexual selection. "Fate has ordained that almost every point on which we differ shd. be crowded into this volume."

Darwin saw "moral sentiments" as following the laws of natural selection: "It can be hardly disputed that the social feelings are instinctive or innate in the lower animals; and why should they not be so in man?" In *The Descent of Man,* published in February 1871, he declared that man, in all his facets, could be descended from the apes.

Wallace, reviewing *The Descent of Man,* disagreed, stating that Man's "absolute erectness of posture, the completeness of his nudity, the harmonious perfection of his hands, the almost infinite capacities of his brain, constitute a series of correlated advances too great to be accounted for by the struggle for existence of an isolated group of apes in a limited area."

Although Wallace's "little heresy" of admitting the presence of a Greater Power caused an intellectual rift between him and Darwin, both he and Darwin shared, at least publicly, the belief in the possibility of the refinement of man.

Natural Affection

I do not know if my parents knew—how could they have known?—that on Friday and Saturday nights my friends and I drank cheap blackberry wine, bought for us by our Lansman's camp counselors for $1.99 a bottle. We took our stash to the campgrounds, which were to us far from the world the adults inhabited inside the darkened casino way past the other side of the pool. I knew that on these nights, my brother worked late as a waiter at a nearby hotel. I had the one-bedroom bungalow to myself. Drunk or not I could bring Paul, or another one of my longtime Lansman's friends, back for sex.

Although it was at Lansman's that I had my first girlfriend, it was also at Lansman's where I fulfilled my boyhood fantasies of having sex with my male friends. We moved from pajama parties and changing into our swimsuits in the same room to games of strip poker and jumping naked over the campfire during sleepouts in the woods. Robust sexual experimentation lasted year after year, not ending until we were through our first years at college. To this day, I am amazed by how easily I was able to have sex with friends who, except for youthful summer sessions in which they willingly played their part, never had sex with a man. Or did they have sex with each other? How many of them thought they were the only one doing these things with me? Was it attraction we felt for each other?

Now, I wonder what my childhood friends, most now married, think of those unclothed hours we spent together. I never felt shame about my early sexual encounters with my friends. Did they? I wonder if they ever talked about those nights. Or was I the only one who knew?

I kept up with these friends long after I told them and started writing about my homosexuality. Did my being gay somehow make them question their own sexuality? Remembering those nights, how do they now feel about the sex we once shared? Would any of my childhood friends consider that these experiences put them in a category called, if not homosexual, then bisexual?

Finally, in what category should I be placed? I was, after all, involved with a girl named Vicki that long-ago summer at Lansman's when I was also having sex with my male friends in a bungalow that no longer exists except in my memory.

Wallace's Survival

In the 1868 *Proceedings of the Zoological Society,* T. H. Huxley named the biogeographical boundary between Pacific and Asiatic species "Wallace's Line." That same year, a medium was publicly attacked as a fraud and Wallace collected testimonies, as well as giving his own, as evidence to disprove the attacks. Returning from a British Association meeting in Glasgow, Hooker reported that "Wallace as Presiding Spiritualist made a black ending to a scientific meeting." Darwin and his friends wondered whether Wallace would prove, in the end, a liability to the growing science of evolution.

In 1871, Wallace decided to draw on his experience as a surveyor, and began building a house, Dell, in the village of Gray, on the north bank of the Thames, twenty miles east of London. His son, William, was born in December 1871. Dell was finished in March 1872. In 1874, Bertie, aged six, died. Arabella Buckley, secretary to Lyell and an amateur medium, assured Wallace that Bertie was being taken care of by his uncle Herbert.

Like Darwin, Wallace dealt with his grief by immersing

himself in his work. In 1876, his two-volume *Geographical Distribution of Animals* was published. *Nature* called it "the first sound treatise on zoological geography." Darwin said the book would be the basis "of all future work on Distribution."

Building Dell was yet another financial drain on Wallace. Architects and builders cheated him. In 1880, he sold the house and moved his family to a small cottage in Godalming, where he hoped to live on the meager earnings of his publications. He began secretly assisting Lyell for five shillings an hour. Darwin considered helping Wallace by hiring him to edit the second edition of *The Descent of Man*. However, although Darwin had supported other friends in their research and projects, as well as when calamities struck, he never directly assisted Wallace with money. Instead, he planned to get a government pension for Wallace. "I hardly ever wished so much for anything in my life as for its [the pension's] success," Darwin wrote to Arabella Buckley. He used his connections to Prime Minister William Gladstone to attain the granting of the pension. "It has been an awful grind—I mean so many letters," Darwin told Buckley. He also enlisted the support of Hooker who, at first, did not support the plan. Hooker believed Wallace had "lost caste" and would be an embarrassment to the scientific fold.

Wallace's *Island Life,* which looked at island animal and plant speciation, was dedicated to Hooker and published in 1880. Darwin thought the book "Quite excellent," deeming it the "best book" Wallace had ever published. Hooker said Wallace had "brushed away more cobwebs that have obscured the subject than any other author." Hooker told Darwin "that such a man should be a Spiritualist is more wonderful than all the movements of all the planets." Hooker, after the publication of *Island Life,* added his support for Wallace's pension. The Duke of Argyll, a member of Gladstone's cabinet, also supported the plan.

On January 6, 1881, Gladstone wrote to Darwin: "I lose no time in apprising you that although the Fund is moderate, and is at present poor, I shall recommend Mr. Wallace for a pension of 200 pounds a year." Darwin immediately wrote to Wallace, telling him that "twelve good men" had supported the pension. He hoped this would give Wallace "some satisfaction to see that not only every scientific man to whom I applied, but that also our Government appreciated your lifelong scientific labour."

Wallace greeted the news as a "joyful surprise." He thought the modest pension would provide "very great relief from anxiety" for the rest of his life. He replied to Darwin: "There is no one living to whose kindness in such a matter I could feel myself indebted with so much pleasure and satisfaction."

wheelchair

Disability Made Me Do It

In 1991, I am living in Provincetown when I get a call from Tom, a local artist. Tom has been hired to do the drawings for an updated version of a well-known guide to gay sex. "I want to make sure different types of men are represented in the drawings," he begins. "I wanted to talk to you about how to best portray a disabled man having sex."

"Don't use a wheelchair to signify the man is disabled," I tell him.

"Where can I find a disabled guy to model for me?" he asks.

"Beats me," I say.

"Would you do it?" There is a pause. "I'll take photos of you having sex and use them as the source for what I'll draw," he explains.

"Sex with whom?" I ask.

"That's easy," Tom assures me.

Why did I so easily agree to model for the cause?

In 1988, I was working for a San Francisco theater services organization when I was asked out to lunch by a man interested in getting to know his way around the theater community. "I was an understudy in *A Chorus Line*," the man tells me as we sit down for what I expect to be a business lunch. "What can you tell me about directing a play in San Francisco?"

Over salad I tell him what I know about getting a start: classes, the theaters, some people I suggest he call.

After the waiter removes the plates from the table, my lunchmate looks across the table at me and asks, matter-of-factly: "Do you like to be humiliated?"

I know right away what he is talking about, where this conversation is leading, even though no one has ever asked me that question before. "Why do you ask?"

"Because I know this one guy in Los Angeles who told me that's the only way he can enjoy sex. Pain and humiliation bring up all the times he got attention when he was a kid, so he gets off on it."

For me the operative words are *this one guy in Los Angeles*. I could answer him by pointing out how many nondisabled men, gay or otherwise, enjoy experiencing sex that way, or offer him other enlightened responses, but at this moment all I can muster in reply is, "Really?"

In 1990, a nondisabled gay male editor who is interested in my work takes me out to lunch at a ritzy New York restaurant.

"I was very interested in the sex in your book," the editor tells me.

"Oh?" I say. As I eat I keep nodding encouragement for him to continue.

"I have a cousin who is disabled. We spent a lot of time together growing up in Texas," he says. "My family wasn't very happy about how swishy I was. We lived in oil country and I guess I didn't live up to, well, what they expected a boy to be. My cousin was my only friend. People are very interested in how disabled people have sex, aren't they?"

Puzzled, my first thought is that not many people would be interested in the way I have sex, being that my sexual practices are probably similar to the experiences of most gay men. My unspoken response is: No, most people aren't interested but you obviously are.

Taking into consideration that I might have to work with this well-intentioned man sitting across from me, and that he is paying for this rather expensive lunch, I simply correct his assumption: "Actually, most people do not think of those of us who live with disabilities as being sexual at all."

The Origins of Desire

Who knows the origins of desire?

"In matters of sex," sexologist Albert Kinsey observed, "everything you can possibly imagine has occurred and much that you cannot imagine."

Although the instinct for procreation and survival of the species most often explains the desire for procreational sex, there have been a myriad of explanations for homosexual desire. To Western science, homosexuality, both in animals and humans, is an anomaly, an unexpected behavior requiring some sort of explanation, cause, or rationale. But to many indigenous cultures around the world, homosexuality is a routine and expected occurrence in both humans and animals. Biologist Bruce Bagemihl has shown that a good deal, if not most, of heterosexual sex in both animals and humans is without procreative intent. Thus, homosexual sex is not so different from most heterosexual sex. Except for the cultural context that labels it so.

Similar to its attitude toward homosexuality, our culture demands explanations about most disabilities. The writer Joan

Tollifson, who has one arm, has likened the question "What happened to your arm?" to a koan/mantra that follows her through life. Throughout my life, friends and strangers have asked me "What happened to your legs?" There was a time earlier in my life when I, too, could not stop asking why at birth I was missing bones in my legs. Chance, the fuel of natural selection, was not at that time a satisfactory explanation.

Disability studies theorist Lennard J. Davis echoes Bagemihl, showing how, when we speak of disability, we associate it with a story, place it in a narrative. A person *became* deaf, *became* blind, *was born* blind, *became* quadriplegic. The impairment becomes part of a sequential narrative.

By doing this we think of disability as linked to individualism and the individual story. What is actually a physical fact becomes a story with a hero or a victim. Disability becomes divorced from the cultural context, and becomes the problem of the individual, not a category defined by the society. The dialectic of normalcy—for someone to be normal, someone has to be not normal—is kept intact.

The Imperfections of Beauty

To St. Augustine, "beauty was synonymous with geometric form and balance." Regarding human appearance, the *Oxford English Dictionary* defines *handsome* as: "having a fine form or figure, usually in conjunction with full size or stateliness." Psychologist Nancy Etcoff describes the historical discourse on beauty as "an aesthetic based on proportion."

When I was young, before we went to sleep, my brother, three and half years older than I and with whom I shared a trundle bed, teased me about how short I was. "I'm not short," I replied, "everyone else is tall."

Now, when I wake during the night, I am surprised when I realize my body, lying so closely to Ian's, is of measure. Because above my thighs my body is of customary length, lying in bed with him I feel the equality of my body's size. I feel comfortable, at ease, something I do not feel when standing up and talking to someone at a party where I often don't reach anyone's shoulders, or when sitting down for dinner in a restaurant where usually my feet dangle from the chair, unable to reach the floor. In crowded elevators I am often unseen, relegated to a back corner where the view is more often the middle of someone's back, or below.

In 1991, the night before Tom's photo shoot, I begin to get nervous. I have not taken off my clothes, been naked and shared my body with a stranger for many years.

I can't sleep. Lying in bed, I think about the story of Thai Queen Number One. Thai kings were polygamous; each queen had a number according to her station. A long time ago, Queen Number One was on her way to visit the king in the ancient capital of Ayutthaya. It was a very hot, humid day and Queen Number One decided to stop at the river.

As she cooled off in the river, the queen's servants watched over her royal possessions. Suddenly, the queen began to drown. Because no subject was allowed to touch a queen, number one or otherwise, her servants were relegated to simply stand and watch her from the shore. Did any of the onlookers know Queen Number One could not swim? She drowned.

The next morning at Tom's studio, I am told the part of the book that I will model for will be "Biting."

That doesn't sound too heavy, I think to myself, as I introduce myself to George, my partner for the session.

Even though it probably wouldn't have made me any less nervous, I wish I had asked Tom if he had told George about my disability before we met. Next time remember to ask, I tell myself, as if this session will be my first step in what is sure to be a nude modeling career.

I don't know George well enough, have never seen him until a few minutes ago downstairs—has he ever seen me and my inimitable gait walking down Commercial Street?—to ask if he has ever done this before. What I do know is that he has olive skin, tight curly black hair, dark brown eyes.

"Why don't you two get to know each other?" Tom says as he checks a light he's set up over the bed.

And before I can give Tom's suggestion a moment's thought, George has trampolined onto the bed and is pulling me toward him.

Here in bed it feels as if the playing field has been literally leveled. Despite my insecurities, even though a half hour earlier I did not know George, I am soothed by his fingers grazing my shoulder, the length of my arm.

Later that week, Tom calls. He wants me to come over to look at the photos, as well as at the drawing he has already begun.

When I see the photos and drawing at his studio, I am both surprised and relieved by my reaction. I recognize the images of myself in both the photos and the drawing as very beautiful.

A week later, Tom calls. "The art director didn't like it. He said that in the drawing the disability didn't read. He wants me to cut off one of your legs."

"My parents didn't let many well-known doctors do that when I was born," I tell Tom.

"Or I can put in a wheelchair by the side of the bed."

"But that's the easy way out. We talked about this before I agreed to model."

"I know we did."

"What are you going to do?"

There is a long pause.

"I can put somebody else's head on your body, then take off one or both of your legs," he offers.

"You can't do that. If you can't use my body as it is you can't use my body at all."

In 1993, the book on gay male sex is published and no drawing of me is included. Instead, accompanying the section on "Masculinity" there is, included in a drawing of a group of otherwise nondisabled men, one fully clothed man sitting in his disability-signifying wheelchair.

As I stare at the drawing, I realize that a man with a disability has once again been defined *as* his disability instead of being portrayed as a person *with* a disability. To the large audience who will use this book, this might be the only image they will ever see of a disabled gay man. And the message of the drawing: "Despite his having to use a wheelchair, he is a man, too," rather than "Here is a man who also uses a wheelchair."

Leaving the bookstore, I am sad at this missed opportunity.

Waking the next morning, I get out of bed, reluctantly. Who was I kidding? I ask myself as I get up to take a shower. Was modeling for Tom any different from my earlier sexual encounters?

Feeling the strong pulse of the spraying water run over me, I close my eyes and it is as if the water's heat slowly dissolves the skin of my limbs, then my bones, until I am one of those armless, legless, Greek statues—all torso—something akin to a male *Venus de Milo* who, despite having no arms or hands, the stump of her upper right arm extending just above her breast, despite her scarred face and severed left foot, despite having the big toe cut off her right foot, and a missing left nipple, not being real, is considered one of the most beautiful figures in the world.

earthworm

The Accumulation of Little Things

In the late 1870s, Darwin began researching what caused plant roots to turn downward. In November 1880, he published *the Power and Movement of Plants.* Then he turned his attention to worms.

Darwin wanted to learn how long it took worms to bury stones as they upturned the earth. He was convinced that worms were intelligent: a worm could find the midpoint of a leaf to fold it into two halves. Emma described her husband as "training earthworms, but [he] does not make much progress, as they can neither see nor hear. They are, however, amusing and spend hours in seizing hold of the edge of a cabbage leaf and trying to pull it into their holes. They give such tugs they shake the whole leaf."

Darwin's final book, *The Formation of Vegetable Mould Through the Action of Worms,* was published in October 1881. In the preface he cautioned: "The subject may appear to be an insignificant one." But the principle of his research, "small agencies and their accumulated effects," had remained the same

since his *Beagle* voyage. Darwin, since experiencing the Concepción earthquake in 1835, believed the story of nature could
be explained by the "accumulation of little things." In his last
book, his use of his prior knowledge and earlier research, his
extensive use of the research of other naturalists, anatomists,
and specialists from England and abroad, proved once again his
own description of himself as "a kind of machine for grinding
laws out of a large collection of facts."

Darwin died on April 19, 1882, at the age of seventy-three,
and was buried in Westminster Abbey. Wallace, then fifty-
nine, was a pallbearer at the funeral.

Shoes in a White Cardboard Box

Finally, Jim calls to tell me the new shoes have arrived.

"Did they take care of my shoes?" I ask, more concerned about my familiar pair than any new ones.

"They're a bit dusty from the plaster," he tells me.

The next morning I am back in the strip mall office. First, I want to see my old shoes. When he takes them out of a white cardboard box, they look paler, as if they have aged. Touching them, I flake off what I assume is plaster from the casting molds and remember how my father replastered my casts when I was a boy.

"Here are the new shoes." Jim hands me the new, lightweight pair to try on.

"They look nothing like the old ones," I say, trying them on. I get up and walk around. So far, so good. "Seems like more support, but I won't know until I start to wear them."

"Take them home and let me know," Jim says, holding up his crossed fingers.

Driving home with my new shoes, I don't have high hopes.

The next day, when I go to the bank and run some other errands, I slip, almost falling face down on the sidewalk. Still, returning home I keep my new shoes on for an hour more. The next day, my right knee buckles, my hip and back begin to ache.

I keep at it for a three more days until, finally, I can no longer walk. That night I repolish my old shoes.

The next morning, my feet are back inside my polished old shoes. I put the new pair in the white cardboard box, stash it in my bedroom closet, on top of the LPs I no longer use.

Living Among Them

Wallace believed that if everyone had an acre of land, a million people would rise from poverty. During the 1870s, when Wallace had taken up land reform, Darwin hoped that he would not "turn renegade to natural history."

To help pay for his son William's college tuition, Wallace began to lecture at schools. In the fall of 1886, he was invited to Boston to give lectures at the Lowell Institute. He accepted the offer, proposing a lecture he called "The Darwinian Theory," and three others on color in animals and plants. He decided to expand his lectures in Boston, and to tour America.

In various cities across the country, Wallace met with many American spiritualists. In one Boston séance, a short old gentleman with white hair and a beard was conjured. The man took Wallace's hand and bowed. At first, Wallace thought it was Darwin, but then recognized the man as his cousin.

On January 11, 1887, Wallace lectured at New York's American Geographical Society on "Oceanic Islands: Their Physical and Biological Relations." He wanted to see Niagara Falls, so he scheduled lectures in Canada. He followed in Lyell's footsteps, lecturing in Cincinnati and visiting the burial mounds in the Ohio Valley. He passed through St. Louis and Kansas City before lecturing on Darwinism in Lawrence, Kansas. He reached Oakland, California, on May 23, 1887. Soon after his arrival, he took a trip to the redwoods with conservationist John Muir.

During his last days in California, Wallace developed a swollen upper lip that required lancing. After a week's recuperation, he headed to the Sierra Nevada to collect botanical specimens. The highlights of Wallace's American sojourn were the Bay Area redwoods and the sequoias of Yosemite:

> Neither the thundering waters of Niagara, nor the sublime precipices and cascades of Yosemite, nor the vast expanse of the prairies, nor the exquisite delight of the Alpine flora of the Rocky Mountains— none of these seem to me so unique in their grandeur, so impressive in their display of the organic forces of nature, as the two magnificent 'big trees' of California. Unfortunately, these alone are within the power of man to destroy, as they have been already partially destroyed. Let us hope that the progress of true education will so develop the love and admiration of nature that the possession of these altogether unequalled trees will be looked upon as a trust for all future generations, and that care will be taken, before it is too late, to preserve not only one or two small patches, but some more extensive tracts of forest, in which they may continue to flourish, in their fullest perfection and beauty, for thousands of years to come, as they have

flourished in the past, in all probability for millions of years and over a far wider area.

To Wallace, "the big trees" were like the birds of paradise: "[T]heir majesty grows upon one by living among them."

Spilled Rice

Born in 1967, Ian is the son of an Irish immigrant mother and a German immigrant father. He is six-one, blond, has bright blue eyes. He reads a lot, paints, draws, creates videos, and makes a living as a Web designer. He likes to watch sports just as much as I do. Every Labor Day, we go together to the U.S. Open tennis tournament in Flushing, Queens.

Ian, during his last year in graduate school at Columbia University, is living in a loft in the Williamsburg section of Brooklyn. I've come from Massachusetts to go with him to watch the tennis tournament. It is Saturday morning and I'm all ready to leave the loft to catch the train to the USTA Tennis Center. Ian seems just about ready to go, as well.

Having known Ian for over a year, I now know to give ourselves plenty of time in the morning so we aren't late. Last year, Ian was diagnosed with attention deficit disorder (ADD). Since then, he has taken Ritalin. Throughout his life, Ian has tended toward lateness, has had difficulty completing projects, is constantly losing things like his keys and wallet.

I glance at the clock: 9:15 A.M. I calculate that it will take us fifteen minutes to walk to the train. We'll have to take the L train into Manhattan, then transfer to the Lexington Avenue line, and finally, at Grand Central, transfer to the number 7, which will take us to the tennis center. If we make all the transfers without waiting, the ride will take us about an hour. If we leave now, we should get to the tournament with a few minutes to spare.

"Ready?" I ask Ian.

"Just about," he says as he reaches for his backpack.

I open the door and go outside into the hallway, assuming Ian will be right behind me.

"Where are you?" I call into the loft.

No answer.

I go back inside and find Ian, seemingly all set to go, in the kitchen.

"What are you doing?" I ask.

He is holding the bag of rice that has been on the counter at least since the last time I was here over two weeks ago.

"Putting the rice into the container," Ian says as he opens the paper bag and begins siphoning the rice into a glass jar.

"Do you have to do it now? We'll be late."

"I've been meaning to do it for a while."

"We've got to go."

"Hold on."

"Let's go, Ian."

"It will only take a—"

The bag of rice has torn, and what seems like millions of grains of rice cascade onto the counter and onto the kitchen floor.

My first reaction: anger that we'll be late to the U.S. Open. But then I see that Ian, using one hand as a broom, his other hand as a dustpan, is on his knees cleaning up the rice. His hands are shaking. He has begun to cry.

"It's okay," I tell him.

"I'm such a fuck-up," he says, sitting down on the floor.

I sit down with him amid the spilt rice.

"Why did I have do the rice now, just before we're going to leave. I saw it there and I couldn't let it go."

ADD

"Finding out I had ADD was such a relief," Ian says. "It explained to me so much that happens in my life and how people, including my parents, have reacted to me since I was a child."

ADD has been defined as a "neurological syndrome whose classic defining triad of symptoms include impulsivity, distractibility, and hyperactivity or excess energy." According to this definition, ADD is not a learning disability, a language disability, or dyslexia. Clinically, it is not associated with low intelligence. In fact, many people who have ADD are very smart.

Some see ADD and the use of Ritalin, the most prescribed medication associated with ADD, as a symptom of "modern life" rather than a symptom of a "modern disease"—as the inevitable byproduct of a culture addicted to speed: cell phones, beepers, overnight mail, powerful computer chips, hard-driving rock music, TV shows with images spliced together at hundredth-of-a-second intervals.

Another theory relates to dopamine, a chemical in the brain.

It is thought that dopamine plays a major role in attention and inhibition. Performing certain tasks or taking part in a complex social situation generates dopamine in parts of the brain that deal with higher cognitive tasks. If you looked at a thousand people at random, you would find a huge variation in their dopamine systems, just as you would if you looked at their blood pressure.

According to this theory, ADD is used as a label for people whose dopamine falls at the lower end of the scale, the same way we say that people suffer from hypertension if their blood pressure is above a certain point. In this context, to get normal levels of attention and inhibition, a person has to produce normal levels of dopamine. Ritalin is a drug that affects the neuroreceptors, allowing the amount of dopamine available for cognition to remain higher than it would be otherwise.

Critics of these theories about ADD think that if someone needs a drug in order to be "normal," then the problem is with our definition of "normal." Physician Lawrence Diller: "What if Tom Sawyer or Huckleberry Finn were to walk into my office tomorrow? Tom's indifference to schooling and Huck's 'oppositional' behavior would surely have been cause for concern. Would I prescribe Ritalin for them, too?"

To some, like Malcolm Gladwell, that's just the point. He points out that Huck Finn and Tom Sawyer lived in an age where difficult children simply dropped out of school, drifted into poverty and violence. He criticizes Diller for romanticizing what Gladwell calls a ruthlessly Darwinian world, which provided only for the most economically—and genetically—privileged. We now place children in situations in which these children can't be cast aside because of "some neurological quirk" that causes them difficulty in coping.

To proponents of Darwinian medicine, which looks at

medicine from an evolutionary perspective, just as the evolutionary example of walking upright gives us the ability to carry food and babies, as well as predisposing us to back problems, many of the genes that predispose us to mental disorders may have fitness benefits, as well. Many of the environmental factors that cause mental disorders are likely to be specific aspects of modern life, and many of the more unfortunate aspects of human psychology are not flaws but "design compromises."

Sickle-cell anemia is an example of a disease caused by a gene that is also useful. The gene that causes sickle-cell disease occurs mostly in people from parts of Africa where malaria has been prevalent. A person who inherits this gene from one parent gets substantial protection from malaria, because the gene changes the hemoglobin structure in a way that speeds the removal of infected cells from circulation. However, someone who inherits this gene from two parents gets sickle-cell anemia.

Because such protection from malaria increased the likelihood of reproduction and gene replication, the sickle-cell gene was selected in a particular population. Now, even though those Africans who no longer live in malarial zones do not need such protection, the gene is still present in the genome.

This situation is also similar with the gene for Tay Sachs disease, a gene present in 3 to 11 percent of Ashkenazi Jews, which provides a relative immunity to tuberculosis, and the gene for cystic fibrosis in some Scandinavians, which at younger ages helps protect against such diarrheal diseases as cholera.

It is easy to forget that humans evolved into their present state in a completely different environment: the ancient hunter-gatherer societies.

If ADD has a genetic component, then what advantage could this gene have provided to have been naturally selected? People with ADD are the leftover hunters, those whose ancestors evolved and matured thousands of years in the past in hunting societies.

In such societies, traits such as constantly monitoring the environment, the ability to change strategy at a moment's notice, visual thinking—all of which are attributed to those with ADD today—would be advantageous. Those ADD "hunter" types have compensating characteristics, such as voracious curiosity, continual scanning of the environment, and broad-based interests. If our schools and jobs were structured to allow for the expression of these characteristics, ADD might become as irrelevant a medical classification as its reciprocal.

In a differently structured world, ADD would not be a disorder but merely one in the vast array of possible behaviors.

A Gap in the Wiring

The train ride to Flushing for the U.S. Open is quicker than I had planned. Ian and I make it to the tournament on time.

But ADD makes Ian's navigation through his last year of graduate school more difficult. His move to Brooklyn from Manhattan adds a considerable amount of travel time between home and school. No longer can he impulsively drop in for a nap at his old apartment a few blocks from Columbia. He is unable to prioritize his own work with the time necessary to fulfill the duties of his fellowship as director of the digital media center. If either is neglected, he is threatened by the department chair.

Even after his diagnosis and his receiving accommodation from the office of disabled student services, Ian's progress to his graduate degree does not go smoothly.

Soon after Ian's diagnosis, I read Allyson Goldin's article on special education in *The New Republic*. Goldin, a former special education aide, writes about one of her students:

Here is his missing link, the gap in his wiring where
rhyme should connect to reason. That synaptic elec-
trobond is just not there, and it won't be taught into
existence any more easily than a one legged man can
be taught to have two legs. I am irritated by people
who believe all . . . disabilities can be 'outgrown' in
time or remedied by purchasing a few books-on-
tape. . . . Brains don't reconstitute themselves with
any more frequency than legs do.

*Brains don't reconstitute themselves with any more frequency
than legs do.* Ian is late; I can't do steps. Ian can't finish his
drawings; I can't go food shopping on my own. I realize I've
never had a relationship with a disabled man before.

A Young Man in a Hurry

Returning to England, Wallace collected his lectures on natural selection for a book, *Darwinism: An Exposition of the Theory of Natural Selection with Some of Its Applications,* published in May 1889. He knew his view on man would be criticized:

> I (think I) *know* that non-human intelligences exist—that there are minds disconnected from a physical brain—that there *is,* therefore, a spiritual world. This is not for me, *a belief,* merely, but *knowledge* founded on the long-continued observation of facts—and such *knowledge* must modify my views as to the origin and nature of human faculty.

In the 1890s, Wallace proposed creating a society based on equality of opportunity: providing the fullest and best training possible to both sexes until the age of twenty-one, followed by three years of industrial service to ensure each individual's proper choice of occupation. Everyone would receive a common share of public "credit" to alleviate poverty.

Here, Wallace struggled with the same issue that he grappled with in his first writings on natural selection: how to reconcile survival of the fittest with his belief in the improvement and perfectibility of humans. Now, he saw that "the survival of the fittest is really the extinction of the unfit," but that the process in the case of man had been checked by "the essentially *human* emotion" to save the weak and the suffering, a trait antagonistic to our physical development but crucial to our moral development. Wallace saw this dilemma as pitting our animal instincts against our human instincts. His answer was to eliminate poverty and leave the rest to our "cultivated minds and pure instincts."

Despite Wallace's outspoken, socialist, and unconventional views, he continued to be lauded. In 1892 he received both the Founders' Medal of the Royal Geographic Society and the Royal Medal of the Linnean Society. In July 1908, in honor of the fiftieth anniversary of the reading of the Darwin-Wallace papers, the Linnean Society held a celebration. A medal with busts of Darwin and Wallace, one on each side, commemorated the event. Wallace described this as an "outrageous attempt to put me on a level with Darwin!"

At the event, he described his discovery of natural selection, comparing himself with Darwin: "*I* was then (and often since) the 'young man in a hurry': *he,* the painstaking and patient student seeking ever the full demonstration of the truth he had discovered, rather than to achieve immediate personal fame."

Wallace accepted the medal "not for the happy chance through which I became an independent originator of the doctrine of 'survival of the fittest,' but as a too liberal recognition . . . of the moderate amount of time and work I have given to explain and elucidate the theory, to point out some novel application of it, and (I hope I may add) for my attempts to extend those applications, even in directions which somewhat diverged from those accepted by my honoured friend and teacher Charles Darwin."

By the autumn of 1913, he had grown weak, suffering from arthritis. He made little progress on his proposed book, *Darwin and Wallace*. On November 2, he felt ill and went to bed. One newspaper mistakenly printed an obituary the next day.

Alfred Russel Wallace died at the age of ninety on November 7, 1913. His modest family declined to have him buried in Westminster Abbey, burying him in Broadstone Cemetery in Dorset, where he had spent the last fifteen years of his life.

black monkey

Black Monkeys

The day after Ian and I visited the Bali Starling Reintroduction Center, we are back in Bali Barat National Park. This time, after an early morning rain, we are here to see the black monkeys. Unlike the sacred gray monkeys that, as guardians of the Balinese forest temples, are ubiquitous, the rare black monkeys are only found here, where they are protected in what remains of the Balinese jungle in the northwest corner of the island.

Our guide takes us into the dense jungle. The trees are still waterlogged from the rain and, every few steps, drops fall on us, and I am again that eight-year-old boy searching in the woods behind my family's bungalow at Lansman's. But now I am searching for black monkeys, a more difficult task than hunting salamanders.

After we cross an almost dry streambed, I see Ian, strides ahead of me, quietly beckoning our guide. When I reach them, Ian motions for me to be quiet. I stand still, not wanting the noise from my uneven gait to scare away what he has found.

Ian points to a tree.

This scene will be repeated many times throughout the afternoon: Ian, ahead of me beckoning to the guide, motioning me to be as quiet as I can be, pointing to where only he can see what we have come to see: an entire family of rare and endangered black monkeys.

In the jungle, Ian's brain is firing on all cylinders, full of color, sound, light, and movement, just as it always is. But here in the environment from which we have evolved, only through his eyes can I finally see what I have come halfway across the world to see.

With drops of water still falling from the leaves onto my head, I look where Ian directs me. He sees yet another family of monkeys. Finally, through the trees, I see one large black monkey staring back at me.

Here, in our world we share together in the Balinese jungle, the hunter helps the starling.

Perverse Nature

Darwin said, "All nature is perverse and will not do what I wish it." He knew that nature and its laws could not be controlled.

Wallace's break with him concerning the origins of man shows that not everyone was in agreement with all that Darwin thought. Some disagreed and drew different conclusions. Others focused on one aspect of Darwin's theory of natural selection, taking it out of context, spawning many variations, most notably Social Darwinism and eugenics, which took aspects of Darwinian thought and used them for purposes of social engineering.

Herbert Spencer, the philosopher who first used the term "survival of the fittest" and championed evolution before and after the publication of *On the Origin of Species*, was the chief proponent of Social Darwinism. Spencer publicly advocated that government and other institutions refrain from regulating social conditions: "To aid the bad in multiplying is, in effect, the same as maliciously providing for our descendants a multitude of enemies." He believed that social institutions should not "put a stop to that natural process of elimination by which society continually purifies itself."

The global economic recession of the 1870s encouraged the view of societies in competition in a hostile world. In the United States, business leaders such as Andrew Carnegie believed that unrestrained competition was natural selection at work. Human intervention could not mitigate the struggle for existence.

In the United States toward the end of the nineteenth century, Social Darwinism transformed into eugenics. Whereas Spencer and the Social Darwinists advocated a laissez-faire policy, supporting the status quo of the economic and social hierarchy, eugenicists advocated an active governmental and institutional role in "purifying" society of perceived "weakness."

In 1881, Alexander Graham Bell, inventor of the telephone, researched deafness in Martha's Vineyard, Massachusetts. He concluded that deafness was hereditary. In "Memoir Upon the Formation of a Deaf Variety of the Human Race" he recommended a marriage prohibition for the deaf. He warned that boarding schools for the deaf could become breeding grounds for a deaf human race. In 1896, Connecticut became the first state to prohibit the marriage between anyone who was "epileptic, imbecile or feeble-minded."

By the 1880s, European studies stressing the heredity of criminality had become the basis for "criminal anthropology" in the United States. In 1887, the superintendent of the Cincinnati Sanitarium issued the first published recommendation of sterilization for criminal activity.

Race increasingly became a focus for eugenics. Darwin rejected the idea that different races were different species. Racial differences could not be explained by natural selection because "none of the differences between the races of man are of any direct or special services to him." To Darwin, race was outside of evolution.

However, Darwin's Victorian view of a hierarchy of different cultures fostered racist conclusions to be drawn from his work. In 1904, sociologist William Elwang wrote: "The trouble with the negro is not merely that he is ignorant. The difficulty is more radical and lies embedded in the racial character, in the very conditions of existence. The negro race lacks those elements of strength that enable the Caucasian to hold its own, and win its way and bring things to pass. Negroes cannot create civilizations." Similar statements about the innate inferiority of women were also common.

In 1905, soon after French psychologist Alfred Binet developed a test for mentally deficient school children, psychologists and social scientists in the United States began mental testing on a large scale. In 1907, Indiana passed the first state law allowing the sterilization of "confirmed criminals, idiots, imbeciles, and rapists" if a committee of experts judged that procreation was inadvisable. By 1915, thirteen states had passed similar laws; by 1930, a total of thirty had enacted them.

In 1910, biologist Charles Davenport received funds from the Carnegie Institution to found the Station of Experimental Evolution. He became director of the Eugenics Records Office in Cold Spring Harbor, New York and lobbied in favor of immigration restrictions.

Eugenicists became "expert advisors" to the U.S. Congress on the threat of "inferior stock" immigrants from Eastern and Southern Europe. In 1924, Congress passed the Immigration Restriction Act, reducing the number of new immigrants by 15 percent to control the proportion of "unfit" individuals entering the United States.

In 1927, the U.S. Supreme Court decided *Buck v. Bell*, a case centered on the constitutionality of a 1924 Virginia law allowing the involuntary sterilization of those in state institutions who were deemed feebleminded. Justice Oliver Wendell Holmes Jr.'s majority opinion said that "experience has shown that heredity plays an important part in the transmission of insanity, imbecility, etc. . . . Three generations of imbeciles are enough." Holmes's opinion was signed by all but one of the nine Justices. Between 1907 and 1963, more than sixty-four thousand individuals were forcibly sterilized under eugenics legislation in the United States.

After the stock market collapse of 1929, it became difficult to believe the correlation between economic status and intelligence. During the Great Depression of the 1930s, social scientists shifted their emphasis to the social causes of human difference.

The realization that the Nazis in Germany were putting into practice many of the ideas of eugenics also contributed to the shift toward a social definition of difference. As late as January 1934, American eugenicist Paul Popenoe defended the Nazi program of sterilization of the "eugenically deficient." A favorable report by Popenoe on the results of sterilization in California was cited by the Nazi government as evidence of the humaneness and feasibility of wide-reaching sterilization programs.

In 1934, 56,000 persons with mental and other "defects" were sterilized in Germany. By the middle of 1936 the number had risen to 150,000. In 1939, the Children's Program, the first killing program designed to eliminate Germany's disabled, began. Between 1940 and 1941, T-4, the adult killing program, was responsible for killing at least 275,000 German adults with disabilities. All of this led to the Final Solution, now known as the Holocaust.

Darwin did say that "the weak members of civilised societies" propagate and "this must be highly injurious to the race of men." However, he quickly qualified his statement by also saying that "the aid which we feel impelled to give to the helpless is mainly an incidental result of the instinct of sympathy, which was originally acquired as part of the social instincts, but subsequently rendered . . . more tender and more widely diffused. Nor could we check our sympathy, even at the urging of hard reason." He concluded, "If we were intentionally to neglect the weak and helpless, it would only be for a contingent benefit, with an overwhelming present evil. We must therefore bear the undoubtedly bad effects of the weak surviving and propagating their kind."

In the United States, as early as 1888, anthropologist John Wesley Powell, who had lost an arm in the Civil War, responded to Spencer and the social Darwinists: "Man does not compete with plants and animals for existence, for he emancipates himself from that struggle by the invention of the arts; and again, man does not compete with his fellow-man for existence, for he emancipates himself from the brutal struggle by the invention of institutions." Sounding more like Wallace, Powell disagreed with Darwin's belief in the continuity between animal and human evolution. He believed "human evolution arises out of the endeavor to secure happiness; it is a conscious effort for improvement of condition."

Anthropologist Franz Boas, a German Jewish immigrant who came to the United States in 1882, provided the groundwork to refute Spencer and eugenics. In 1887, Boas wrote of his experience with Eskimos, refuting the common stereotype of "primitive" peoples: "[T]he mind of the native enjoys as well the beauties of nature as we do; he expresses his grief in mournful songs, and appreciates humorous conceptions." He collected Eskimo songs and texts, and found that "though most explorers affirm that their music is nothing but a monotonous humming," the examples he collected showed this was not true. "That the mind of the 'savage' is sensible to the beauties of poetry and music, and that it is only the superficial observer to whom he appears stupid and unfeeling."

Boas, echoing Darwin, rejected eugenics outright by stating that it ran counter to human nature, because to think that human beings could regulate their procreative behavior in support of socially determined goals was ridiculous.

In the United States, Boas was active in leading social scientists to oppose the racism of the Nazis. In 1938, the American Anthropological Association unanimously passed a resolution denouncing racism. The resolution stated that anthropology provided no scientific grounds for discrimination against "any people on the ground of racial inferiority, religious affiliation, or linguistic heritage." Rarely had a scientific body passed such a resolution.

After the war, when asked why eugenics declined so quickly in the United States, Popenoe admitted "the major factor . . . was undeniably Hitlerism." But as early as the 1880s, reformers such as Powell and Boas spread Darwin's message that no one stayed on top, because change and adjustment were the order of nature. Boas, invoking the Darwinian notion of constant change, asked: Was it possible that traits thought to be desirable today, would be viewed otherwise in the future?

Aqua Booties

Aqua Booties, Size Six

Ian enters the fitting room carrying a tower of shoeboxes in his arms. In less than a week I am scheduled for a fifteen-day whitewater rafting trip down the Colorado River through the Grand Canyon. We've already found the right wetsuit in the local sporting goods store. Now we're trying to find the wetsuit booties that will fit my feet.

I have visited the canyon twice before. Crowds poured out of their RVs to watch the picture-postcard sunset from folding chairs, families screaming at one another in the heat. I couldn't walk all the way down from the canyon rim to the Colorado. Grand Canyon National Park was not one of my favorite places. But now, here was the chance to experience the canyon the way I had always wanted to, by being right in the middle of it.

When I received the flier announcing the trip, it stayed on my desk. When I woke up in the middle of the night, I would go into my office and see it staring back at me. The trip was for the disabled and their friends. I wouldn't be the only disabled person going. But Ian had to work and couldn't go with me.

Who would set up my tent, carry my gear, help me get to the places I wanted to go? I would need to wear my shoes on land, but needed them to be kept safe and dry when on the river. The kayaking I did in Thailand was in calm water. How would I keep my shoes dry, safe from the rapids of the Colorado? If they were lost or damaged how would I get home? How would I survive without them?

Finally, I called. On the phone, Mary McDonald, the trip organizer, assured me that my shoes could be kept safe and dry. Dry bags and sturdy metal boxes would be on board the boats. A volunteer guide would help me with all the physical tasks that I couldn't do. "That's what they're there for," she assured me.

Mary also told me the Colorado has very cold water, no more than fifty degrees. When I told her I have difficulty immersing myself in the water of a heated pool, she suggested I bring a wetsuit and booties.

Because of my short legs and my leg length discrepancy, since I was a child all the pants I buy need to be altered. Until I was a teenager, my mother conscientiously cut and hemmed. Then, a local dungaree store that did alterations on site kept my measurements—19 inches for the left pant leg, 17 1/4 inches for the right—on their alteration room wall. Now, I take my pants to a local tailor called Sew Good. But a wetsuit made of neoprene, a cross between spandex and rubber, cannot be altered. How would I find a wetsuit that fits me?

Mary, used to dealing with all sorts of bodies, suggested I look for a type of wetsuit called the Little John. This wetsuit has a full-size top connected to wetsuit pants that are like shorts. As for the booties, she suggested one size for one foot and another size for the other.

It was good to talk with someone who understood my dilemma, but I still never thought I'd find the proper gear. I felt despondent. Hopeless. But to Ian, who has neither my fear, nor my legs, finding the gear for my trip was an adventure.

Looking through the wetsuits in the sporting goods store, we found the Little John. Gradually my fear and embarrassment abated. The Little John was, as Mary had suggested, the answer. Now, here was Ian with his tower of boxes, bringing me every wetsuit bootie in the store that he thought might fit my feet.

"I've got all kinds and all sizes," Ian tells me.

Ian begins to open the boxes. A new wave of hopelessness rises from my stomach to my chest. How could someone with my body even think about rafting down the Grand Canyon? Fear, long entrenched, does not dissipate easily. I feel like a fraud.

Ian bends down to put a bootie on my foot and I cannot help imagining Prince Charming. But if he is Prince Charming, then I am Cinderella, still embarrassed at fleeing the ball. No slippers, glass or otherwise, will slip easily onto my feet.

"Let's try the ones with zippers down the side first," Ian says. "One with a rubber sole for support. Let's fit your left foot first. And let's start with the smaller sizes."

It is as if we are back in the Bali jungle, Ian deftly spying the black monkeys, leading me through the dense trees. Miraculously, the first one we try—an Aqua Bootie, size six—fits my left foot.

"Stand up. How does that feel?" he asks.

Standing up, I am sure that the bootie on my left foot will cause my foot to hurt. But to my surprise, I am able to hold my weight. "Amazing," is all I'm able to say.

"Now, maybe we should try a smaller size for the right, but let's see if the right one will fit, as well," Ian says looking up at me with his smile.

He hands me the other bootie. I cannot believe it, but it fits, too. Standing up and walking around, I know, will be the true test. I do not want to injure myself. I keep expecting my right foot, without the support of my shoe, to roll over on its side.

But, again to my surprise, the zipper, the Velcro strap, and the rubber sole keep my foot upright. The neoprene bootie has the right combination of flexibility and support. My knee does not buckle. I do not fall. In the small fitting room, I walk from wall to wall.

"How did you know these would work?" I ask Ian.

"I guessed. I know your feet pretty well by now," he says, still kneeling on the floor. "You're a size six. How does it feel having your own shoe size?"

I have no idea how to answer.

Foaming Over It

The night before departing for the Grand Canyon, I watch a PBS documentary on John Wesley Powell's exploration of the Colorado. If that's what the rapids look like on a fifteen-inch television, I know I'm in trouble.

On April 4, 1862, Powell was fighting in the Civil War battle at Shiloh. His right arm was smashed by a cannonball. Three days later in Savannah, his right arm was removed above the elbow. The PBS narrator reads from *Beyond the Hundredth Meridian,* Wallace Stegner's biography of Powell: "Losing one's right arm is a misfortune; to some it would be a disaster, to others an excuse. It affected Wes Powell's life about as much as a stone fallen into a swift stream affects the course of the river. With a velocity like his, he simply foamed over it."

Later, I try to fall asleep. Fear and anticipation keep me awake. I keep telling myself that Powell made his trip through the canyon with one arm. Images of rapids, more like surf, become larger and larger throughout the night. Even if I wasn't disabled I'd still be afraid.

In my late teens and early twenties, I was not afraid to travel. As a college junior I lived and studied in London and at Cambridge. That year, during school holidays, I traveled through Europe, carrying just a backpack. In 1984, I went to Israel. I've spent weeks searching for ruins in the Southwest desert, traveled with Ian to Bali. I traveled alone in Thailand.

As I get older, it seems fear rises more quickly, more forcefully. I become anxious as I get closer to leaving home. "If there are people born without the capacity for fear, you might well look for them in the emergency room or the morgue," say Drs. Nesse and Williams in *Why We Get Sick*. "Fear is the signal that a situation may be dangerous, that some kind of loss or damage is likely, that escape is desirable." So, why is fear showing up now that I'm older?

I've inherited from my parents perseverance, as well as the fear of imminent danger. As I get older, these competing instincts to strive and retreat cancel each other out, and I become more conflicted the closer I get to the time of departure.

Still awake, I think about Eli Clare, a writer with cerebral palsy who loves climbing mountains. Clare writes about confronting the image many people have of the disabled: the "supercrip." This image has saturated the world with stories about "gimps" who participate in activities ranging from the grand to the mundane: a boy without hands bats .486 on his Little League team, a blind man who hikes the entire Appalachian Trail, an adolescent girl with Down syndrome who learns to drive and has a boyfriend. These stories focus on disabled people "overcoming" their disabilities, reinforcing the superiority of the nondisabled body and mind. The writer Joan Tollifson, writing about her life with one arm—"People tell me with tears in their eyes how amazingly well I do things, such as tie my shoes"—shows how these stories turn disabled people, who are simply leading their lives, into symbols of inspiration, from individuals into abstractions.

Like Eli Clare who loves the mountains with a "deep down rumble" in his bones, I love to travel. And like Eli Clare and many other disabled people I, too, carry the myth of the super-crip. It is often too difficult for me to separate what I want to do from what I cannot do. I am confused by the commingling of my fear with my desire.

With a velocity like his, he simply foamed over it. I think about John Wesley Powell, one-armed, running the Colorado River in a wooden dory no bigger than a rowboat; how Powell climbed up the rocky side of a canyon only to find himself alone on a ledge, unable to get down. I think about how once I walked up the Mountain of the Lion and the Lamb in the Lake District in England; how I finally made it to the top. With my legs and back aching, I barely had the energy to get down. I think about my fourteen-mile descent from Glacier Point down into Yosemite Valley. Not realizing it would take me so long, I had to navigate the final three miles of the trail limping in the dark.

Still not sleeping, I want to wake up Ian to tell him I'm not going.

I get out of bed to read Stegner's words about Powell, the words I heard on the video: *Losing one's right arm is a misfortune; to some it would be a disaster, to others an excuse.* Looking up, I see my bags ready to go by the front door. I know at the bottom of the duffle bag is my wetsuit and my Aqua Booties. Next to my backpack is my only pair of shoes.

Back in my bedroom, Ian is sleeping comfortably on his side of the bed. I remember him walking into the fitting room balancing, barely, the tower of boxes of wetsuit booties.

I look out the window and realize I have not slept all night. It is already dawn.

Reciprocal Altruism

"We are now ready to start on our way down the Great Unknown. Our boats, tied to a common stake, are chafing each other, as they are tossed by the fretful river," John Wesley Powell wrote as he began his first trip down the Colorado River.

I look around at the diverse bunch we are: Mark, Daniel, and Hanna use wheelchairs. Ben and I use canes; Sally and I have orthopedic shoes. Six of the eleven participants have disabilities ranging from quadriplegia to multiple sclerosis; our ages range from midtwenties to midseventies. "Although it might sound corny, we're going to be living as a family for the next fifteen days," Bert, our trip leader, tells us before we put in on the river.

Among us are seven guides from Environmental Traveling Companions (ETC) who will assist those who need assistance. There are also six guides from the commercial companies, one in charge of each of four yellow rubber boats, and two who run the larger motor rig that will carry our gear, the food, as well as the wheelchairs, downriver.

Day 1. We take it slow, rock layer by rock layer descending into the canyon. Quickly, I adapt to life on the river: the difficult mobility on sandy beaches; going to sleep and waking up early; al fresco toilets. I learn how best to sit in the boat, using a padded backrest that not only lessens the strain on my back but, when tied to the boat's rigging, gives me something extra to hold onto.

Most important, I develop a preboarding routine. I pass my shoes and cane, wrapped tightly in a black trash bag, to Matt and Tim who run the "big rig," where they keep them in a long, rectangular metal box. When we stop for lunch, I see the black bag waiting for me by a white plastic chair. When we stop to camp for the night and I again see the black bag waiting for me by the chair, the fear of losing my shoes begins to lessen.

The morning of Day 2. In Marble Canyon, we make our way through the Roaring Twenties, a series of fierce rapids, getting our first hit of the forceful waves. The water is colder than I imagined. Since this part of the canyon runs north–south, we are not exposed to much sun.

Rafting through the Roaring Twenties, Bob, my boatman, trains us to lean to one side of the boat when he says to do so. "High side," he shouts, and those who can, lean toward the right front side of the boat. I watch Bob's developed upper body maneuver the oars through the spiraling water, allowing us to make it safely through the first set of rapids. I begin to trust him and want to be assigned to his boat each morning.

By the afternoon I am able to relax, absorb the geological information of the stained dark red walls of this part of the canyon. I lose myself in the sheer immensity of a place where a sense of scale and distance easily disappears.

Day 3, late morning, we reach Vasey's Paradise, an oasis of greenery fed by a narrow waterfall high on the river right canyon wall, named by Powell after a botanist. Here, everyone gets out of the boat. Guides Ray and Steve carry Hanna, a woman with multiple sclerosis who needs assistance to move, into the flow below the waterfall. The flow, coming from a side canyon, is cold but not as cold as the water in the Colorado.

After much hesitation, and much exhortation from my river companions, I decide to venture forth onto the slippery rocks. This will be my first experience walking with my wetsuit booties on land. Looking at the rocks, I try to gauge how much assistance I might need: someone to help me get out of the boat; someone on each side to steady me on land. I ask Ray and Steve for assistance, and with their help I make it to shore.

I am not used to walking without my thick-soled, heavy leather shoes. The wetsuit clings to my body. It is difficult to focus on walking when I am surrounded by blossoming trees—a surprise in the desert—the green seemingly darker by contrast to the red canyon walls.

I watch the water flow down the walls into the clear side canyon stream, then into the muddy Colorado. After my first few steps out of the boat, I no longer need Ray and Steve's assistance. Now it is as if I am walking weightless on the moon.

That night, after dinner I sit with Mary and the guides by the campfire. I thank Ray and Steve for their help in getting me out of the boat into Vasey's Paradise. I ask Ray, "Why do you do this?"

"I have a cousin with cerebral palsy. And I love being on the river."

William D. Hamilton, a British biologist, was the first to link Darwin's assertion that natural selection may be applied to the extended family. Since members of a family share the greatest amount of genes, altruistic behavior toward family is in the gene's replicative self-interest. A gene that repaid kindness could spread through the extended family, and then, by interbreeding, to other families.

"I find most guides have experiences with a family member or a close friend who is disabled," Mary tells me.

Vishnu Schist

The Schist

Day 6. After Bob guides the boat through Hance, a technical feat due to the large rock that must be avoided to run the rapid, we enter the schist, and it is as if we have landed inside the earth's core.

The Vishnu Schist, exposed in the Inner Granite Gorge is metamorphic rock, which forms the oldest, deepest layer in the Grand Canyon. This black rock comes from lavas, sandstones, and siltstones that accumulated on the floor of a Precambrian sea over 1.7 billion years ago. The schist is some of the oldest exposed rock known to man. The pink and red Zoroaster granite provides relief as it veins its way through the dark schist.

It is believed that life has been present on earth for at least 3.4 billion years. But until about 2 billion years ago, this life was anaerobic and unicellular. Just before the metamorphosis of the Vishnu Schist, living organisms with chlorophyll created a new free-oxygen atmosphere. This atmospheric change caused wide-scale extinction of anaerobic forms and made multicellular evolution possible.

This morning, floating through the schist, I once again think of Darwin after the Concepción earthquake, before he reached the Galápagos, making the connection between Lyell's piece-meal geological elevation and what he saw before him. And like Darwin during his expedition in the Andes, I am awed not only by what I see, but silenced by the realization that here—floating on the Colorado River through the Grand Canyon—I am transported back through unfathomable time to the moment before everything we now know as life happened.

The boatmen pull up their oars. All of us are silent. The only sound is the current of the river, the sound of being taken wherever the river will take us.

A Portafloor and Yellow Boats

John Wesley Powell is the first person with a disability recorded to make his way down the Colorado River and through the Grand Canyon. The six of us with disabilities on this trip are not the first disabled people to make the trip since Powell.

In the early 1970s, the National Park Service (NPS) implemented a system to control river access, issuing a certain number of user days to commercial companies plying the river. The NPS was petitioned by a group of Arizona outdoors enthusiasts with physical impairments. In 1972, these activists demanded user days for the disabled and started a group, called Jumping Mouse Camp, to go downriver.

Day 7. Another hot day. "Take a look at this," calls John, the owner of Outdoors Unlimited, one of the commercial companies leading our group down the river.

I move closer to an ashen green, thick stub of a flowering plant close to the ground. With his index finger John touches the pistils in the center of its bright pink flower. When he gently moves his finger the petals of the flower begin to close.

"The prickly pear cactus thinks my finger is an insect large enough to pollinate it. So, the flower wants to capture me long enough to make sure I will spread its pollen to another flower. Quite an adaptation for desert survival."

At lunch, I talk with John, who has come on the trip to learn more about the kinds of adaptations people with disabilities need on the river. "Besides a close friend of mine, there haven't been too many disabled people on our trips," he tells me.

"I wouldn't want to be the only disabled person on a trip," I say. "I'd feel as if I'd be holding up the group if I took extra time. And I'd feel a bit sad that I couldn't do everything everybody else was doing."

We walk back to the boats on the modular plastic strips arranged on the sand in various configurations so wheelchair users can maneuver more easily on the uneven ground. "I was at a wedding, one of those backyard affairs in a tent," John says, "and I saw them using these Portafloors to even out the ground in the tent and provide paths outside on the lawn. My friend in a wheelchair wanted to make a trip down the river with us, and I thought these would be the perfect thing to make it easier for him on the sand." So, the Portafloor is not made by ETC, as I'd assumed, but an existing invention John adapted for their use.

Day 9. Late on a clear star-filled night. I sit by the river. With no mirror, with only a flashlight and a small bucket of cold water, I shave for the first time since we launched above Marble Canyon.

As I shave, I think about how on this trip the rule is: if everyone can't do it, nobody does it. So far, despite our impairments, and because of adaptive uses of such items as the Portafloor and the help of the guides, we have been able to do almost everything done by a group without disabled rafters.

Almost everything on the shore is an adaptation: not only

the portable flooring but also the makeshift kitchen, the pump system with which we purify our drinking water, the outdoor toilets, the bucket I'm using for cold water outdoor shaving, even the tents, the light I see moving inside Sally's tent, and surely the yellow rubber boats. All are adaptations that allow as many people as possible to run the river as safely and comfortably as possible.

Here I am, sitting and shaving on the banks of the Colorado River in the Grand Canyon. Outside the tents, the three wheelchairs reflect the moonlight. Inside their tents, Daniel, Mark, and Hanna are probably asleep. Sally is still moving around her tent, organizing her gear.

I walk to my tent. Before I go to sleep, I polish my shoes.

Crossing the River

There are different ways to cross the water.

Day 10, and we have reached Havasu Canyon. Today, my aim is to make it only half a mile up the canyon to sit amid the pink rock and clear aquamarine water of Havasu Creek.

The four yellow oar boats are moored side by side just inside the mouth of the side canyon. To get from our boat to the shore, I have to cross over the other three anchored boats. From the boat closest to shore, I can see that big-riggers Matt and Tim have left the black bag containing my shoes and cane three hundred feet away on the rock ledge, my initial destination. Good thinking. When I reach the ledge, I sit down and change from my wetsuit booties into my shoes. Looking at the uneven path through the rocks, I'm glad I polished my shoes last night.

As I change into my shoes, another group of adventurers passes by.

"We're just so impressed," a frosted-haired woman stops to tell me.

"Don't be impressed," I hear myself say. "Read my books."

Boatman Dan and his wife Kate, who joined the trip two days ago at Phantom Ranch, will accompany me up the canyon in case I need assistance.

On the rocky trail, I am able to maneuver using only my cane. But as we continue up the canyon, the rocks become larger and larger until the path is almost impassable. A quarter-mile up the canyon, boulders block the way. There is no longer a path on this side of the creek.

"You'll have to cross the creek to get up the canyon," Dan tells me.

How do I cross the water? My choices: (1) I can change back into my wetsuit booties, which I've wrapped in the black trash bag and put in my backpack, and make the crossing myself; (2) I can change back into my wetsuit booties and ask for help across the water; (3) I can ask Dan to carry me across.

Darwin, in *The Descent of Man,* talks about how, as man's reasoning powers improved, each individual would soon learn that if he aided others he would receive aid in return. From this "low motive" he might acquire the habit of helping others. In turn, this habit of performing benevolent actions would strengthen the feeling of sympathy, which then would become the initial impulse for more benevolent actions.

I decide to ask Dan to carry me across the water.

On the other side of the creek, the trail continues. A short hike up, I find a rock ledge to view lower Havasu Canyon.

"You go on ahead," I tell Dan and Kate. "Pick me up on your way back down."

Lying down on the rock, I use my backpack as a pillow. The midday sun blurs the boundaries of the water, the rocks, the sky. Aquamarine blends into pink into blue. Where have I seen something like this before?

All of a sudden I see Ian on the ledge of the Beehive on

Mount Desert Island and I think how, in the great majority of situations in my daily life, I am the most disabled. But when I climbed the Beehive with Ian, and on this trip, I've been the most able.

I look up-canyon and see Sally, maneuvering on her rocker-shoes. Sally has been far more active on the trip. She has asked for less help than I. But I have noticed Sally spends much of her free time organizing her gear, has not slept well at night, and is constantly tired.

Although I have missed Ian very much—his ADD-self would thrive out here hunting for a place to camp and gathering our gear—I have also been glad he is not with me. When we are together, especially when we travel, the physical labor usually falls to him. This trip has given me the opportunity to test my physical limits, as well as my emotional strength. I've been able to experience how I no longer push myself too much.

But I still feel uncomfortable not only needing help but also asking for it. Often the feelings of fear and shame are even worse after I get assistance. It seems easier somehow when I'm paying for someone to do something for me. Even though I paid for this trip, I know the guides are volunteers. I want to trust their assistance, as well as the mere offer of it, more than I do.

Darwin's journey toward the theory of evolution itself was an act of reciprocity. His social situation, his finances, his family and friends, led to his collecting success, as well as to the publication of his theory. He used his family members in his experiments, and was assisted by neighbors. To arrive at the ideas at the core of *On the Origin of Species,* Darwin depended on the theories of others, such as Malthus, Lyell, and Wallace. Was Wallace's lack of social standing the reason he is not remembered today for cofounding evolutionary theory?

As man advanced in civilization, Darwin noted, small tribes

became united into larger communities. Each individual began extending his social instincts toward all members of the tribe and eventually to members of the same nation, even though these people were personally unknown to him. Darwin concluded that once this point was reached, only artificial barriers prevented an individual's sympathies from extending to the members of all nations and races.

Is this what people with disabilities offer to society: an example of the importance of interdependence, of community? Is this how people with a physical difference help the human species survive?

We're going to be living as a family for the next fifteen days. Despite sounding corny, trip leader Bert's words have been borne out by our journey. We have reached this point not only as individuals but as a community of twenty-five rafting downriver.

Looking up the canyon, I see Dan and Kate. Soon, it will be time to cross back to the other side of the water. This time there will be no hesitation in how I get across.

Once again, Dan carries me and it is as if I am that four-week-old infant being carried out of the incubator. Needing and accepting assistance is leading me toward a great unknown, a journey as immense as the history of the layers of rock and the river that helps form all that surrounds me.

Radiant, Not Blinding, Light

The early morning sun reflects off the driveway through my bedroom window. Occasionally, I hear a car pass slowly down the street. It must be between six and seven o'clock in the morning. I cannot tell whether I have been awake or asleep the past few hours. All I know is that I am extremely tired. The coolness of the sheets on my feet reminds me I am back home in my bed.

The past two months, I have been unable to put my left foot on the ground without pain. From my bed, I can look out at the empty driveway. I see the just-risen sun reflecting off the asphalt outside my bedroom window. I close my eyes, take a deep breath, then another, my usual way of trying to reduce my rapid heartbeat. I begin to count my breaths: one, breathe in breathe out; two, breathe in breathe out—a simple meditation with which I am sometimes able to calm my body—three, breathe in breathe out; and when I open my eyes—*am I dreaming?*—the orange-robed monks I watched each morning in Bangkok are making their procession up my driveway.

Without looking, I know each monk, every one of them, is not wearing shoes.

My driveway is Rama IV, Silom, Yaowarat, all the streets of Bangkok, all the streets of Thailand where every early morning over a hundred thousand orange-robed, barefoot monks walk on *bintabaht* through village and city streets, carrying only their *baht,* black alms bowls, in which families, young and old, place rice and curries, for the monks to take to eat back at their monasteries. This is their only source of food.

This daily morning ritual is the same throughout Thailand, except at Wat Benjamabophit, the Marble Temple, in Bangkok. Here, the faithful bring the food to the monks who wait in the tree-shaded street in front of the temple before taking their food inside, where an hour later I imagine they will eat their curried rice on the smooth, cool, gray marble that distinguishes this temple from all the thousands of others throughout Thailand.

I get out of bed and put on the padded slippers, child-size, bought from GapKids, to wear around the house and minimize the pain in my foot when I'm cooking. I go to my bedroom closet, slide open the closet door. My LPs are still wrapped, bound together with newspaper, an easy way of transport devised when I moved to Northampton. On the top shelf: a white cardboard box. Instantly, I remember that last attempt at having new shoes made, now over three years ago. I take down the box and open it. In the hours between midnight and dawn, I put on what I thought then would be my new shoes.

Slowly, making sure my left foot doesn't hurt, I walk through each room of my house, putting on the lights. When I reach the kitchen every light in the house is glowing, refracting off the yellow-gold walls.

Standing in the kitchen in my would-be new shoes, I am taller. I see corners of the kitchen counters I don't usually see. I open a cupboard and I reach up to a shelf I usually can't reach. Eye to eye with the toaster oven, beneath the latticed metal tray, I see the looped metal elements. When I turn the toaster on, the elements slowly turn a deep orange and I realize that this appliance that I have taken for granted is not a given but it is an adaptation for the way we live now. So is the refrigerator, the stove, even the table and chairs—all that evolutionary backache we avoid by not sitting on the ground—in the middle of the room.

Plates, gold to match the color of the walls, ceramic bowls, also gold, forks and knives—I'm opening all the drawers—cups, mugs, and glasses, water pitcher, empty recyclable bottles.

I'm in my office: the computer, the fax machine, bookshelves, the calendar, the books, the printed letters on the books' pages. The living room: the television, the carpet, the sofa—evolutionary backache avoided again—the lamps, the candles.

The bathroom: the towels, the soap, shampoo, the toilet, the sink, the shower, the plumbing invisible inside the walls. The sewage system. The electrical wiring. Everything in my entire house—the entire house itself—everything as it is, but everything an adaptation.

The bedroom: the phone, the newspapers and magazines, the windows, the double-arched bed—backache once again avoided by adaptation. But a sharp pain travels from my left foot up my leg. I know it is time to take off my shoes.

Back to the closet. Again, the LPs. For the past ten years of very little use. Vestigial organs.

I put away the shoes.

It is now past dawn and I am exhausted. Back in bed I close my eyes and wonder if the orange-robed monks are again traipsing up my driveway. Bright orange changes to burnt orange and the old blind monk-priest dressed in his burnt orange robes. I wonder if he is still alive.

As if in answer, the old blind monk gives way to another elderly man: the aging artist Henri Matisse.

Why Matisse? What's he doing in my bedroom?

Darwin: "[E]ach of us at some period of life, during some season of the year has to struggle for life and to suffer great destruction."

In 1941, Matisse was seventy-two. Cancer surgery had left him with a prolapsed stomach so he had to wear an iron belt, making it increasingly painful for him to stand for more than an hour at a time.

Two years later, stones in Matisse's bile duct triggered jaundice that, from time to time, caused him to stay in bed for long periods of time. Many times, he woke up in the middle of the night and, awake in bed, remembered the past. The cutouts of 1943 are the first works that Matisse, confined to his bed, worked on at night.

How could he paste his gouache-colored cutouts on the paper so high on his studio wall? Unlike the photographic record of FDR, there are many photographs of Matisse in his wheelchair. There are also photographs of Matisse's assistants helping him with his work. Darwin: "Each man would soon learn that if he aided his fellow-men, he would commonly receive aid in return."

Always interested in the border between drawing and color, Matisse began "to draw in color," replacing the brush and pencil with scissors during the last decade of his life.

His experience with the cutouts spiritually rejuvenated him. He saw the advantage of having had both his illness and the surgery, saying it made him feel young again. He didn't want to take for granted his new lease on life. To Matisse, this was a second life, and the work he did before his illness and surgery "smacked of too much effort." In his new work, he felt he represented himself as free, detached.

Matisse likened this second life to flying, as a plane trip "helps both to forget and to find peace of mind which makes everything possible." He was surprised by the feeling of motionlessness and great security. It seemed impossible to fall.

What mattered to him was "to find joy in the sky." This is "the radiant but not blinding light" with which he longed to infuse his work. His bodily impairment gave him the impression that he was indeed floating in this radiant light throughout the remainder of his life.

Somewhere in these hours I know that I, like Matisse, can adapt to the circumstances in which my body places me. Like Matisse, I can learn from my disability experience. Darwin: "No one supposes that all the individuals of the same species are cast in the very same mould. These individual differences are highly important for us, as they afford materials for natural selection to accumulate."

As the world's various cultures continue to evolve, who knows what will help us survive?

Shoes and the Calvaria Tree

The calvaria tree was an endemic species of the Mauritian forests. The seeds in the calvaria fruit were eaten by the dodos. The seeds, extracted from pits, were not digested but saved from destruction in the dodo's gizzard, allowing them to be distributed broadly on Mauritius after they exited the dodo's digestive system. Then, in the post-dodo era, these seeds, without the protection and transportation provided by the dodo, were trapped inside their thick-walled pits. By 1973, few calvaria trees were left on Mauritius. What once had been adaptive now was maladaptive.

When I was young, we were all relieved when I finally got my shoes back in time for me to catch the school bus early Monday morning. Only in my father's dream were the shoe-maker's store, and my shoes, set on fire.

As my mother led me from our apartment to the elevator, I, wearing my newly soled and tapped shoes, tried to imitate the dancers I saw in movie musicals. Waiting for the elevator, I smiled as I listened to the rhythm I was making as my shoes echoed down the tiled apartment building hall.

But those shoes are of another time. My body, the context for those long-ago shoes, has changed.

Six months after my trip down the Grand Canyon, the pain in my left foot has me once again thinking of the Ilizarov contraption. I call Dr. Frankel's secretary. She tells me Dr. Frankel has decided to retire and is no longer seeing patients. Two days later she calls me back with Dr. Frankel's referral to Dr. Sally Rudicel at Boston Jewish Hospital. Dr. Frankel thinks highly of her and she is in Boston, closer to where I live in Northampton.

The night before I drive to Boston for my appointment with Dr. Rudicel, I can't sleep. In the Grand Canyon, the sandy beaches are created by side canyons, and the debris from side canyons tends to create a rapid, so we usually camped above fiercely flowing water. Sometimes on the Colorado, when I woke up in the middle of the night, I walked to the edge of the rapid to see what obstacle we would pass through in the morning. Back in my tent, the noisy rapid seemed to get louder and louder each hour I lay awake, my fear once again returning with a force so strong that the rapid water was all I could hear. Can fear once learned be unlearned?

In Dr. Rudicel's hospital office, the secretary leads me to a large examination room. I wait for the doctor. When she enters the room, she is accompanied by a young intern. "Do you mind if he's here?" she asks. "He needs to learn." She winks at me as she smiles.

"He can stay," I tell her. "Do you want to see the X-rays?" I ask, offering her the large envelope I brought with me.

"I'm not sure they'll tell me anything I can't see for myself. What's the problem?"

"I can't put any weight on my left foot without it hurting."

"Take off your shoes," Dr. Rudicel says.

I take off my shoes. As I take off my socks, I notice that the doctor is not looking at me but at my shoes.

"They're old," I tell her.

"Do you mind if I call Tom Coburn, the orthoticist I work with?" the doctor asks. Before I finish shrugging my shoulders, she is on the phone.

As we wait for Tom Coburn to arrive, Dr. Rudicel examines my legs. "There's not much I'd recommend doing for you," she says. "But I'm sure Tom can help."

The door to the examining room opens and Tom Coburn rushes in. Tom, still boyish in his late thirties or early forties, is dressed casually in a yellow-and-brown checked shirt and khaki pants. "What's the problem?" he asks the doctor.

"Mr. Fries will tell you."

Tom turns from the doctor to me. Before I can tell him about my left foot, the phone rings. The intern answers. "For you," he tells Dr. Rudicel.

"Is it okay to leave you two alone? He'll know what to do," she assures me as she leaves the room. The intern shakes my hand and follows the doctor out the door.

I show Tom the place on the inner edge of my left foot that causes the pain.

"Here?" he asks.

I nod. As he presses, the pain causes my foot to jump back from Tom's hand.

"Wow," he says. He holds my left shoe and tries to dislodge the inner mold. "I'd say you've had these for twenty years. Incredibly made."

"I don't think the mold has been taken out since I got them." I'm worried he won't be able to get the mold back into the shoe.

"Here's the problem." Tom shows me the place in the mold that matches the place on my foot where the pain is being caused. "I can solve the problem by cutting off about an eighth of an inch of the mold. Easy."

"An eighth of an inch?" I don't believe him.

"Come downstairs and, while we're at it, I'll mold you for a new pair of shoes." Sensing my hesitation, he adds, "I'm up to the challenge. What do you have to lose?"

Black Shoes

Outside of Dr. Rudicel's office, I find the elevator with access to the basement. In the elevator I see the sign that says, "Press B for Orthotics." The basement hall is lined with pipes. I think about how most oncology departments are in hospital basements. But not here.

When I enter Tom's office, the small waiting room reminds me of my car dealership's repair shop. The oddly shaped room is trapezoidal, as if the entire space was once larger, then cut up irregularly by walls to make an office. I register with the secretary who sits in a raised office behind a sliding glass window.

"Go in there," she tells me, pointing to a door a little to my left behind me. "Tom will be with you as soon as he can."

In the nondescript room behind the door where the secretary pointed, I sit and wait for Tom. A half hour passes and, still not believing an eighth of an inch in the mold will make a difference, I think of leaving. But when I get up and put pressure on my left foot, the pain sits me back down. I take off my shoes.

Finally, the door opens and Tom rushes in. "You made it. I thought I might not see you again." He picks up my left shoe, says "I'll be right back," and is out the door.

Within five minutes, he returns. "Here you go," he says.

As I put on my shoes I look at Tom. My lips and eyebrows question him.

"I told you it would be easy," he says

I take a deep breath and stand up in my shoes. No pain.

"Take a few steps."

I do. Then, a few more. Still no pain.

"Let me get what I need to make a mold for new shoes. Keep walking."

I keep walking, back and forth. Still no pain. I start walking faster, then stamp my left foot with all the force I can muster. For the first time in months I have no pain in my left foot.

"Ready?" Tom asks as he prepares to make the molds. I sit down and once again take off my shoes. He looks at my right foot, jutting out from my leg at an almost ninety-degree angle, for the first time. "Almost unshoeable," he says. "But we'll get it done."

Four weeks later, back in the Boston Jewish Hospital elevator, I no longer need to read the sign, "Press B for Orthotics," to reach Tom's basement office.

"They're black," I say when he brings me my new shoes.

I try on my new shoes and walk around the office. The left shoe is cutting the skin on my narrow Achilles tendon. My right foot rolls over. Tom listens to each problem I'm having with my shoes. Somehow, he figures out where in the shoe— the lift, the mold, or the form of the leather itself—the adjustment needs to be made. He makes the necessary adjustment; I walk around the office some more. He listens. More adjustments. More walking.

For four weeks, twice a week, I visit Tom's basement office and we repeat the process: he watches me walk, he listens to me tell him the problem, he makes the necessary adjustments.

Two months after Tom Coburn first rushed into Dr. Rudicel's office, twelve years after Dr. Frankel told me about the Ilizarov contraption, I leave Boston Jewish Hospital walking, pain-free, in my new pair of black shoes.

The History of My Shoes

At the Smithsonian's National Museum of American History in Washington, D.C., I stare at a rectangular concrete slab. Engraved on the slab is "No. 7." This anonymous grave marker is part of the disability rights movement exhibit I have come to see. The grave is for Bertha Flave, a person with epilepsy incarcerated early in the 1900s at Fairbault State Hospital in Minnesota.

I look at a white cane, accompanied by an explanation that during the 1930s "white-cane ordinances" gave the right of way to blind persons using a white cane in many communities. However, blind people were still barred from restaurants, hotels, and public spaces.

I pass by a "Never T4 again" button, referring to the name of the Nazi program to kill people with disabilities.

I read newspaper clippings from the 1940s about parents of children who began to organize and fight for education and services for their disabled children. Next to the clippings, the exhibition text states that often people with disabilities have had to overcome their own parents' fears and overly protective attitudes.

Above my head is Marilyn Hamilton's quickie lightweight wheelchair. A cover of *Sports N' Spokes* magazine shows Hamilton playing tennis from her chair. At eye level is a "Braille 'n' Speak," an example of how computers have increased access and participation by people with disabilities.

Leaving the exhibit, I imagine one last vitrine that contains an old pair of brown leather shoes.

Disability as Zeitgeist

As I drive from Boston Jewish Hospital onto the interstate, the accumulated fears of my almost-forty years begin to give way to something new I am beginning to understand.

Looking around at all the cars on the highway, I think that humans were not put on earth to drive, and yet here we are, millions of us, all over the world, driving in cars, cruising in boats large and small, flying in all kinds of planes.

The next morning, driving to see Ian in New York, I think of how many doctors thought Dr. Milgram crazy for believing that just because my body did not line up symmetrically around a central spine, it could, over time, adapt to walking. Driving, I understand that Dr. Milgram—like each one of us when we wake up each morning—did not know what might happen, but he trusted in the basic adaptability of the human body, and thus of the human mind. With the assistance of Frank the cobbler, one of the first people I knew who understood the daily impact my legs had on my life, and now, Tom, whose experience, instincts, and ability to listen to what I told

him about my body, combined with the assistance of technology and an understanding of interdependence, adaptations
like my shoes are becoming more commonplace and, as adaptations, natural.

"When you think disability, think zeitgeist," writes disabled
journalist and news broadcaster John Hockenberry.
Humanity's specifications "are back on the drawing board, and
the disabled have a serious advantage in this conversation." We
live in a time when the disabled are on the cutting edge of the
social trend of the broader use of assistive technology. Wireless
technology and electronic gadgets are ubiquitous. The meaning
of what it is to be human is wide open.

Who decides riding a motorcycle is cool whereas riding a
wheelchair is not? Who decides drinking through a straw is
sexy but breathing through a respirator is not? Who decides
using a personal computer is natural but using a Braille 'n
Speak, a variation of a PC, is not?

What we learn by adaptability may tell us more about the
natural ways in which all of us can best flourish in an increasingly interdependent, complex, and confusing world. From
this perspective, the history of my shoes is no more a miracle
than is Tom Coburn cutting an eighth of an inch off my shoe's
mold to alleviate the pain in my left foot; no more a miracle
than is traveling in an airplane across an ocean.

Parking my car near Ian's apartment, I stare down and see
not only my new black shoes, but my feet inside my shoes. I see
not only how my feet have adapted to my shoes but also how
the shoes and the mold inside will be altered by the ever-
altering shape of my feet and legs.

Years ago, when Dr. Frankel told me about the Ilizarov contraption, I thought my evolution had come to an end. Just as
cultures will be forced to reinvent themselves because of

change, just as the fear of the rapids is sure to return the next time I raft down the Colorado, I know that there will be times my impairment, like Ian's ADD, will make it difficult to experience anything but a world of our own making.

red-footed booby

Birds in November

In 2000, two months after my fortieth birthday, I am staring at a red-footed booby. I am on Genovesa, also known as Tower, the large northeastern island of the Galápagos. How strange the web-footed bird looks, sitting on a branch in a short tree.

The red-footed booby, with its grayish bill ending in a patch of red before its blue-patched eye, is the smallest of the three Galápagos boobies. Their black tails distinguish them from other red-footed boobies found in the rest of the world. Ninety-five percent of the red-footed boobies in the Galápagos have a grayish-brown body; the other five percent are white.

Unlike the masked and blue-footed booby, the red-footed is the only booby in the Galápagos that nests in shrubs and trees, building flimsy platforms with twigs and sticks. Their flexible feet are adapted so they can perch on thin branches, up and out of trouble. The female lays one egg, occasionally two, and has great difficulty raising even one chick with her partner as each baby bird needs to be fed for 130 days in the nest. There are only five colonies of the red-footed booby in the archipelago, mostly on the outlying islands where the Galápagos hawk, its main predator, does not fly. Unlike other boobies, this booby fishes far out at sea and uses its large eyes to hunt for food at night.

It is our first full day in the archipelago. Yesterday, after arriving at the airport, we sailed at night on the *Flamingo,* our twenty-passenger boat, north to Genovesa.

This morning, we climbed up through a cut in the island's cliffs. "It's like being on the set for Alfred Hitchcock's *The Birds,*" I say as we walk around the desolate landscape of Genovesa. "Except these birds won't attack us," I add as I realize the thousands of birds we pass, the two types of boobies each in their niche—the red-footed boobies in the trees and bushes; the masked boobies, brilliant white with black wings and a yellow bill with a naked skin mask around their eyes, on the rocks and the ground—do not even react to our presence. Even masked boobies nesting in the middle of the path do not move. We are forced to step off the edge of the path to pass them by.

Later in the afternoon, back on the *Flamingo,* I change into my Grand Canyon–tested Aqua Booties, securing my shoes and cane in a well-sealed dry bag. Due to the strong waves that prevent us from landing on the beach of Darwin Bay, another part of Genovesa, we will have to make a wet landing. From the *Flamingo* we transfer into the *panga,* or dinghy, which will take us closer to shore.

As we approach our drop-off point, I give the dry bag and my backpack to Ian, then lift myself up and fling myself off the front of the boat, landing amid the high tide waves. I wade the rest of the way to the white sand beach, gleaming in the midafternoon equatorial sun.

On the beach, just above the tide line, a sea lion has just given birth to a cub. Two lava gulls land and begin to peck at the fresh placenta, which is still connected to her newborn pup by the umbilical cord, another target for the gulls. Each time the gull pecks, the mother sea lion lets out a loud half-honk, half-groan. She tries to nudge her newborn toward the water, gamely trying to protect it from the birds.

"Where is the father?" I quietly ask Ian. He gestures toward the rocks where a large male sea lion basks unaware in the sun.

All of a sudden a large, red-chested bird flies overhead. "It's a great frigate bird," Javier, our guide tells us. "Look at its distended red chest."

The male frigate bird has a scarlet pouch that, when courting, he inflates into a bulbous balloon. The frigate bird flying with its pouch inflated is a strange sight in late November. This bird is a good three months out of mating season.

"Will he find an interested female to mate with?" I ask.

Javier shrugs and laughs.

"I feel sorry for the bird," I say. "He looks so silly."

Suddenly, I realize I am still wearing my Aqua Booties. If I'm going to walk on land for any length of time, I need to change back into my shoes. I spot my dry bag resting on a lava rock. As I change into my shoes, I watch the lava gulls insistently pestering the mother sea lion and her newborn pup. The out-of-season frigate bird, red chest still inflated, flies another circle in the sky.

Changing the Question

Our second day in the archipelago, I am up at dawn. I leave Ian sleeping in our small cabin and, wearing my GapKids padded slippers, climb on deck. We have traveled during the night to anchor in the bay of Santa Fe Island. Night fog still enshrouds much of the island.

Centuries ago, many ships thought the Galápagos were haunted, even cursed. Because of the fog, many ships could not navigate in the area, getting lost, turning further out in the Pacific. Or so they thought. As soon as the fog lifted, the islands reappeared. Did the ship travel in circles? Did the islands move?

The islands haven't shifted since last summer, even if I like to pretend they have. Stretching out on the chaise longue, I think of our hike up the Beehive on Mount Desert Island in Maine. The view from the top. How much my feet, since then, have shifted, especially my left foot, . . . *a little north, a little south or sidewise* . . .

Taking off my slippers, I feel the small ridge developing on the side of my left foot. I am beginning to walk more and more on this part of my foot. The bow of my left tibia is more pronounced than I remember.

Despite a massage, despite an entire night's rest, my body still hurts from yesterday's exertion. How much longer can I take trips as physically demanding as this one?

On deck, as I fall asleep I wonder if the male frigate bird found a partner who will mate with him out of season.

When I wake—how long was I asleep?—I look out at the bay. My question shifts: How might I continue to be able to take trips as physically demanding as this one?

The fog no longer enshrouds the island.

opuntia cacti

A Cane With No Story

The next morning, we walk up Cerro Dragon, a forested hill newly opened to visitors on Santa Cruz Island. "If we're lucky we'll see the land iguana," Javier tells us. "But we must be quiet. We'll also see the feral goats, which are the reason the land iguanas are becoming more difficult to find. The goats reproduce more quickly than the iguanas and the tortoises. The goat eradication program has not yet reached this island. They eat up all the vegetation that the iguanas need to survive."

We walk up a slight incline through the sparse forest of trees and opuntia cactus. Not even halfway up the hill, we see the goats. Actually, first we hear them, rustling in the brush, then see their hind legs propelling them quickly off the path and into the forest beyond where we can see.

Reaching the top of Cerro Dragon, halfway through our morning's hike, we have not seen a land iguana. At the top of the hill is a view of the *Flamingo,* our boat, anchored in the harbor. In another direction, we see more goats running across the more desolate landscape of the inner part of the island.

As we look out over the island, Javier explains that none of the land iguana species on neighboring Baltra, the point of entry for visitors to the islands, survived the building of a U.S. Army installation, which was turned into the airport. Luckily, some of these species survived because they were brought by an earlier expedition in the 1930s to North Seymour, a nearby island.

We descend from Cerrro Dragon, having almost completed the loop trail, when I notice people in the front of the group have stopped. Walking slower so I don't make too much noise, I reach the group. Ian points to an opuntia cactus at the edge of the brush at the side of the path. There, beneath the cactus, a few months later than the 165th anniversary of Darwin's first encounter with the same species, is what we have come to see: a foot-long yellow land iguana.

The iguana knows we're here. It stares at us. There is a large yellow opuntia cactus flower too high for the iguana to reach. I realize that we have interrupted the iguana's food watch. "The iguana is male," Javier says. "He is waiting for the opuntia flower to fall so he can eat it."

As we watch the iguana take a few methodical steps back into the brush, I wonder how long its wait may be.

Soon, the iguana is barely visible through the brush. I think of the goats, brought here by man, disturbing the ecosystem's balance. How they prance like deer through the forest, not knowing of, and not to blame for, the harm they are causing this yellow prehistoric-looking creature that depends on the island's vegetation for survival. I imagine a herd of goats, grazing from cactus to cactus, devouring every flower before it has a chance to fall.

All of a sudden, I extend my right arm, the arm which holds my cane, toward the brightly colored flower. The end of my cane brushes against the flower, dislodges it. The flower falls to the ground. The iguana sees it—or hears it—fall into the brush. Two slow steps forward and the iguana is munching on the flower. Its bites are just as slow as its movements. It could be fifteen minutes, or more, before it has finished its meal. We do not move until the iguana is sated and has returned among the bush and trees in search of its next repast.

Leaving Cerro Dragon, I wonder if Javier will chide me for using my cane to bring the cactus flower to where the iguana could eat it. We've been told numerous times we're not supposed to feed the animals. What would I say? That I wanted to do my part, however small, to insure the iguanas would be around in another 165 years?

We're back in the *panga* when Ian whispers in my ear, "Without your cane that iguana might have starved."

My cane is beginning to have a story.

Galápagos flightless
cormorant

The Niche of a Flightless Bird

It is the late morning of the fourth day. I am resting after exploring Punta Espinosa on Isla Fernandina, the westernmost and most volcanically active island of the archipelago. The surrounding terrain—new lavas with little vegetation—is carved in black rivers of frozen rock that, when they reach the ocean, form tide pools where young sea lions practice swimming.

The desolate landscape presents, at first glance, a seemingly lifeless promontory of black rock and sand. It is as if time, like the clock in Dr. Mendotti's office during my Social Security disability examination, has stopped.

But the longer I sit here, the more I notice. There are numerous orangish-red sally lightfoot crabs ambling on the rocky shore. A small yellow warbler. A pair of lava gulls. And, all around me—if I'm not careful I'll lean on one of them—are black marine iguanas blending into the black rock, heads up, taking in the warmth of the sun.

Below, in the water, I can see a marine iguana swimming, stopping to eat algae off a partially submerged rock. And turning my head slightly to the right, I see a flightless cormorant emerging from the water.

Larger than all other cormorants, these flightless birds did not get here by walking or wading. Over a long expanse of time, through the process of natural selection, their wings grew shorter and shorter, evolving so they could no longer fly. Now, in the present geological time, the flightless cormorants make their nests in the black lava flows of Fernandina Island, as well as on the western coast of Isabela, the neighboring, and largest, Galápagos island.

All other cormorants are migratory, so they need strong wings to fish in richer waters. But here on Fernandina, the sleek black cormorants, with snakelike necks, stubby wings, and turquoise eyes, are near the colder waters of the Cromwell and Humboldt currents that make the water rich with fish. The estimated 700–800 pairs of flightless cormorants are sedentary.

Piratic frigate birds roam the skies. When a flying seabird returns to the nest, its pouch filled with food for the young, the larger frigate birds attack and do not give up until their victims have dropped their food. The cormorants walk a short distance over the rocks to fish, which not only saves the effort of flying but it is safer for them and their young. The flightless cormorants also have developed a method of feeding their young with half-digested food as liquid pulp, so the frigate birds cannot steal as easily from them as they can from pelicans and boobies.

Sitting here on Punta Espinosa, taking in the sun along with the marine iguanas, watching the flightless cormorant spread its awkward wings to dry in the wind, I know that all around me is what Darwin described as "the little world within itself" where "but in space and time, we seem to be brought somewhat near to that great fact—that mystery of mysteries—the first appearance of new beings on this earth."

blue-footed booby

No Reason

Late afternoon on the fourth day. I am enjoying the cool spray of the ocean as we take an afternoon *panga* ride to see a colony of the other flightless bird, the Galápagos penguin, the only penguin found living in the tropics. Whereas other penguins burrow into soft peat, these penguins, the third smallest in the world, averaging about thirty centimeters high, live in the natural caves and crevices of the lava rock on the coasts of the cooler Fernandina and Isabela waters. In recent years, the penguin colonies of the Galápagos have been decreasing in numbers due to the increase of El Niño weather patterns.

Living with the penguins are colonies of blue-footed boobies. These birds, with their signature sky blue feet and ability to plunge-dive from the sky to fish in the ocean, are best known for their antic mating dance, known to some as "the booby two-step."

"Why are their feet blue?" I ask Javier.

"No reason," he tells me, echoing the answer I have given countless times to people who have asked about my feet.

Big and Small

On islands, mammals tend toward dwarfism; reptiles, toward giantism. Perhaps the most famous giant reptiles are the Galápagos giant tortoises. In front of me, at the Darwin Research Station on Isla Santa Cruz, is perhaps the most famous Galápagos tortoise, Lonesome George.

The archipelago was named after this species, *galápagos* being an old Spanish word meaning "saddle," referring to the saddleback shape of the tortoises' shells. It is estimated that over 200,000 giant tortoises once lived throughout the archipelago. There were fourteen subspecies. Since humans began arriving on the islands, the giant tortoise has become extinct on at least four of the islands. Noted for their slow metabolism and resistance to drought, giant tortoises have been known to live upside down in a ship's hold for over a year without food or water. Females, which are found closer to the shore, were taken in larger numbers than the males, distorting the sex ratio and increasing the rate of tortoise decline.

Lonesome George, a saddleback giant tortoise, was found,

emaciated, on Pinta Island in 1971. The discovery was news; no
tortoise had been found on that island since California
Academy of Sciences explorers killed three in 1906. Lonesome
George, now weighing 550 pounds, dubbed "the man without
a mate" by *Science* magazine, captured the public's imagination
worldwide and helped fundraise for the Darwin Station's con-
servation programs.

When we reach the incubation hut, I am fascinated to learn
that many reptiles do not have a sex gene. The sex of the off-
spring is determined by the temperature of incubation during
a critical stage of development. Warmer nests tend to produce
females; cooler nests, males.

"I can't believe how small they are," I say as we look at the
baby tortoises hatched after at least 120 days of incubation.
"They're smaller than newborn Bali starlings." These tiny tortoises will one day, when released on the island to which its
subspecies belongs, grow up to be, as hard as it is to imagine,
as large as Lonesome George.

waved albatross

Transformation to Flight

The seventh day in the archipelago. Our last island visit is to Española, also known as Hood, the southernmost island. Javier tells us that the mockingbirds on Española are especially tame and are likely to fly onto, and off with, your hat. The marine iguanas on this island have red and green streaks on their backs and heads, making them look like tie-dyed T-shirts. "The iguanas," says Javier, "are this color because the food they eat in the waters off this island is red and green, unlike the diet of the black iguanas we've seen on the other islands."

But this morning all I can think of is the bird that makes this island an especially important place to visit. From April to December, Española is the nesting place for the waved albatross that, except for a few pair on an island near the Ecuadorian mainland, can be found only here. When Javier visited Española a week ago, only a few pair had not yet gone to sea for the season. It is now the end of the first week of December, and he is doubtful we will see the waved albatross, although its nesting grounds are the destination of this morning's hike.

To reach the nesting grounds we need to walk over rock- and boulder-strewn ground. Immediately, I realize my left leg is too unsteady, my right knee too weak, to make it through the obstacle course on my own. I need Ian's assistance. I reach for his hand.

As we walk, slower than I've walked throughout the trip, we pass many large, psychedelically colored marine iguanas. Some lava lizards catch rides on top of the iguanas. We also see another one of Darwin's finches, the cactus finch, a type we haven't seen before.

As we are about to turn inland, we get a close look at the Hood mockingbird when it lands on Javier's shoulder. Another lands on Ian's floppy hat. The one on Ian's hat pecks at it with its heavy bill, then hops down, as does the bird on Javier's shoulder. These birds would rather walk around than fly. Here, they fill the niche of the wader among the land birds of Española.

As we turn inland, the rocks get larger. "I'm not sure I'm going to be able to make it," I tell Ian. "I'm afraid of twisting my foot or my knee."

"Go as slow as you need to." He knows how much I have hoped to see the waved albatross.

Despite our falling behind the rest of the group, we make it across the boulders. Javier and the rest of the group are waiting. When we reach them, Javier shows us a broken waved albatross egg. "The mockingbirds like to peck at the eggs," he tells us. "A few weeks ago, eggs were all over these breeding grounds."

Returning to Española after months or sometimes years at sea, the waved albatross once again finds its lifelong mate. Soon after coming to shore, the birds begin an elaborate courtship, which consists of a complex series of repeated displays: the huge birds face each other and enact the "bill circling," "sky-pointing," "shy look," "drunken swagger," "bill clapping," "mooing," and "gaping." These movements flow into each other and are repeated in varying orders. After short rest periods, the ritual continues once again.

Unlike other albatrosses, the waved albatross does not build a nest. It never stays in the same place for long, sometimes moving its egg, between its legs, some distance. Many eggs are lost and are abandoned. Sometimes, a blue-footed booby, abundant in this area, can be seen sitting on both its egg as well as one abandoned by a waved albatross. Some waved albatrosses do not discern the difference between their egg and another's; and if a pair loses its own, it might "adopt" an egg that has been abandoned.

As we walk toward the cliffs, I fear that this morning I will not get to see what I have come to see. At least I got here. Despite the pain in my left foot and right knee, I am glad to have made the journey. I begin to make my way to the cliffs where I can rest and watch the beautiful and elegant red-billed tropic birds fly effortlessly in the sky.

As I am about to turn away from the nesting grounds I see it: a lone waved albatross waddling awkwardly through the rocky field. The young bird, probably born no more than three or four months ago, is navigating through the boulder-strewn terrain. Its pale head shades to a light yellow on its crown and back of its neck. Except for its dark brown underside and wings, it is white. The large, thick bill is a darker yellow.

I stare at the awkward bird. Its body, a little larger than a chicken's, carries two huge folded wings that, when extended, can span six feet or longer. This waved albatross, seemingly the last one on land this season, is about to fly for the first time. We watch as the bird makes its clumsy way through the runway of nesting grounds, gaining some but not much speed, until it reaches its take-off point near the edge of the cliff where, in an instant, it throws itself off, transforming from a gangly land dweller into an expert flyer.

I run to the edge of the cliff and watch the waved albatross take flight. Its large wingspan makes it as elegant in the air as the tropic birds circling above us in the sky. As I sit and watch the albatross fly from the island, I feel Ian standing behind me, his hands gently massaging my aching shoulders.

Sitting near the edge of the cliff, I realize how difficult this hike has been for my body. But now, as the albatross flies off into the distance, my excitement at what I have just seen overwhelms every other feeling. The waved albatross I saw take off for the very first time will not return to land for at least the next four years.

Infinite Space and Time

It takes an hour to fly from Baltra to Guayaquil on the mainland. I watch the islands begin to recede as our plane ascends into the sky. In my seat on this 1970s-style plane, the question—how might I continue to be able to take physically demanding trips like this?—repeats in my mind.

The difficult physical tasks of the past ten days in the Galápagos—wet landings, walking on sand, hikes up sides of dormant volcanoes, hikes on uneven terrain, even keeping my balance on the *Flamingo*—make me think, once again, of looking at my shoes on the cliffs of the Beehive on Mount Desert Island: adaptation.

But now, after walking with only my cane in Thailand's temples, after kayaking shoeless among the limestone islands of Phang Nga Bay, after searching with Ian for black monkeys in the Balinese jungle, after being Aqua Bootied along the Colorado, after Tom's molding and adjustment of my new black shoes, plus the addition of the GapKids padded slippers to use at home, I realize that because my body keeps changing there is no one perfect pair of shoes. In fact, I no longer have only one pair of shoes. As my body has changed, I now have different kinds of shoes I can use in different situations.

I also realize that eventually I will need to find other ways to take pressure off my body. Eventually, I will get a wheelchair, another "pair of shoes" that will help me answer my ongoing question.

I once again ask: How did I get here? Not only by wearing my shoes but by looking at them. And by looking at my shoes, I now know that the history of my shoes is no more and no less than the capability of change under the duress of culture and time.

"Humanity is but a transitory phase of the evolution of an eternal substance," Wallace wrote, "a particular phenomenal form of matter and energy, the true proportion of which we soon perceive when we set it on the background of infinite space and time."

I am startled awake as the plane touches down on the mainland. Two more planes, Guayaquil to Miami, Miami to Hartford.

Then, the forty-minute drive from the airport to Northampton, where there is a welcome-home package from a good friend and fellow writer who is also disabled. Inside the package: a green T-shirt with four drawings of the evolution from ape to human, the most evolved human sitting in a wheelchair. Underneath is written: "Adapt or perish—C. Darwin."

hand cycle

Epilogue: Sky-pointing

The following spring, one afternoon Ian comes home to tell me the bicycle shop is displaying handcycles outside today. From the shopkeeper we learn that the Massachusetts Department of Environmental Management lends out handcycles every Wednesday afternoon during the spring and summer to people with disabilities.

The next Wednesday, I meet Nancy, who works for the program. Nancy, who had her legs amputated when she was young and has been a wheelchair-user ever since, is an experienced handcyclist. I start out using the simplest model, which is like a tricycle with a larger seat, except you use your hands to pedal forward; reversing the motion to stop.

I never rode a bicycle before. Although I am glad to be able, for the first time in my life, to cycle, I am frustrated that the design of this particular handcycle does not allow me to move at the speed I know my arms can propel me.

"It doesn't go fast enough," I tell Nancy when I return the cycle. "It's frustrating."

"Next week, I'll bring the Easy Flyer," she tells me.

Learning to use the Easy Flyer is anything but easy. Nancy, with Ian's assistance, tries to teach me how to steer the sleek low-riding bike with my butt. The brake is a small lever in the center of the wheel column to which the hand pedals are attached.

As I pedal with my arms, my body wants to tilt with the bike as I make a turn, causing the cycle to run off the road. More dangerous is my instinct to stop the bike by putting my left foot on the ground. I could easily injure my left leg.

"Keep your leg in the bike," I hear Ian and Nancy yell every time I do it.

I've just read an article about how engineers and designers have discovered the body-machine interface is as individual and distinctive as fingerprints. Every person solves problems in his or her own way, with a mixture of technology and body improvisation, the variables being both cultural and psychological. Precise outcomes are hard to predict.

For some reason, I am craving speed. I am determined to learn how to ride this Easy Flyer, and eventually steering the bike with my butt and not tilting my body into the cycle's turn gets a little easier. With each ride I go faster and faster. But Ian and Nancy are still yelling at me not to put my foot down.

"You people with legs are all alike," I hear Nancy laugh after my latest attempt to brake the cycle with my left foot.

But as I start cycling down the path, thinking of Darwin's diverse butterfly collection, I know that what Nancy says is not true. As I begin to become more and more comfortable steering the bike—use butt, keep shoulders straight—I also begin to have more confidence that I will be able to take my right hand off the pedal and stop the cycle by squeezing the small lever when needed.

Soon, Nancy and Ian are in the distance and I am pedaling toward the old railroad bridge that is now used as part of the bike path. Some fellow cyclists on bicycles give me strange, questioning looks. Others simply smile as I pass them by.

Gaining speed, I pass farms and the backs of buildings that, driving on the road, I've only seen from the front. Ahead of me I see the bridge.

On the bridge, the wind off the river feels cooler and I realize I've picked up speed. I've never gone so fast on the cycle before. In the middle of the bridge, I take my hands off the hand pedals and lean my head back so I can see the sky.

I am sky-pointing, I think, and, keeping both feet off the ground, I am the waved albatross, the last remaining bird of its kind, now ready to take flight. I close my eyes and guide myself across the bridge.

Acknowledgments

The author thanks the Blue Mountain Center, Leighton Art Studios at the Banff Centre for the Arts, the MacDowell Colony, the Millay Colony of the Arts, and Yaddo, for residencies during which much of this book was written; the Ludwig Vogelstein Foundation for financial support; the Japan/U.S. Friendship Commission and the National Endowment for the Arts for the 2002 Creative Arts Fellowship, which allowed the testing and sharing of ideas among colleagues in Japan; the staff at the Saratoga Springs Public Library in Saratoga Springs, New York, and the Forbes Library in Northampton, Massachusetts, for assistance in locating research material.

Mary McDonald and the guides of Environmental Traveling Companions, Bob Hart and the boatmen of OARS and Outdoors Unlimited, Sally Walker, and the rest of the group who rafted down the Colorado River through the Grand Canyon; Gede Swastika in Ubud and Frank at the Bali Hati Foundation in Bali, Indonesia, for their warmth and guidance to the right places; John McConville, Bennett Lerner, and Prachan, without whom

Thailand would not have been the same; the late Sarah Petit for the travel assignment to Thailand for *Out* magazine.

Frank and Michael at F&C Shoe Repair in Brooklyn, New York, for tending the shoes since boyhood; Tom Coburn at NOPCO for listening and designing new shoes; Koyo Emma for taking care of the new shoes in Tokyo.

Paul Irving and the many friends whose fortieth-birthday gifts helped make possible the trip to the Galápagos.

Susan Moon for reading the initial essay, "The History of My Shoes," and for the insight that there was much more to tell; Anne Finger whose friendship, wisdom, and editorial eye helped shape early drafts of the book; Elizabeth Wales, who kept with this book for longer than it should have taken; Don Weise for getting it.

Reiko Rizzuto, whose intelligent editorial grace provided the framing of the book's dilemma and whose prodding clarified every chapter.

And most of all, Ian Jehle, for the countless hours, deep discussion, endless love, and editing beyond belief, who lived much of this book—this book is as much his as it is mine.